CHRISTMAS OBSERVED

A Literary Selection

Edited by

OWEN DUDLEY EDWARDS

and

GRAHAM RICHARDSON

POLYGON

ISBN 0 904919 53 6

© Preface, Notes and Selection, Owen Dudley Edwards
    and Graham Richardson.
© "Sundered Hearts", the Estate of P. G. Wodehouse.
© "Christmas in India", The National Trust.
© "The Flying Stars", the Estate of G. K. Chesterton.
© "A Christmas Letter", the Estate of Stephen Leacock.

First published 1981 by Polygon Books,
1 Buccleuch Place, Edinburgh, EH8 9LW.

Typeset in Bembo by E.U.S.P.B.,
1 Buccleuch Place, Edinburgh, EH8 9LW.

Reproduced from copy supplied,
printed and bound in Great Britain by
Billing and Sons Limited,
Guildford, London, Oxford, Worcester.

CHRISTMAS OBSERVED

A Literary Selection

To

THE VERY REVEREND ANTHONY ROSS, O.P.,
Lord Rector of the University of Edinburgh

CONTENTS

PREFACE

OF all festivals, Christmas is both the most derivative and the most individualistic. As a festival with an objective but no clearly set down form, it has evolved in different ways in different places, influenced both by the prevalent style of Christianity practised and by external factors, Christian, pagan and secular. Christ has not scattered the ancient superstitions, as Milton in his "Ode on the Morning of Christ's Nativity" hoped: instead Christmas has assumed superstitions both widely believed in, such as the effects of mistletoe, and also those of more locally based appeal.

Our opening testifies to the diversity of Christmas, with Milton being followed by representatives of the Gaelic Catholic and Protestant episcopalian traditions. Then three different yet intermingled views of Christmas from this century give insights into new questions and old shadows. We move to more traditional prose and poetry, from detection and salvation in Chesterton and Stevenson to the gentle mockery of Wodehouse, Leacock and Arnold Bennett, and the less gentle offerings of Kipling and Saki. We have tried to present less well-known works where a choice from an author was needed: for example, we have excluded Conan Doyle's "The Blue Carbuncle", the only Holmes-Watson Christmas story, in favour of his unknown "An Exciting Christmas Eve". To celebrate classical literary celebration of Christmas it seemed wiser to rely on Pepys, Addison and a paragraph of Macaulay's *History*, all by now better known than read, than to oblige Ebenezer Scrooge to face yet further Christmases to come. But we do stress how conscious we are of great omissions in this

anthology, and hope readers will go from these pages to
rediscover such diverse charms as Dylan Thomas's "A
Child's Christmas in Wales", or Evelyn Waugh's account of
Adam's mad Christmas with the Colonel in *Vile Bodies*. The
latter was a tantalising dish to have to set aside: but although
it has been anthologised in the past, some of its finer
moments only appear in the full context of the novel, and the
same is true of many of the other great Christmases of
fiction.

Christmas has meant sorrow and bitterness, whether in
war or in more intimate tragedy, and literary echoes of those
themes must be heard as well as the joyous or hilarious.
There are the advocates of the abolition of Christmas who
require representation, and our lot here has fallen on an
anonymous Scottish broadside, whose author seems to have
declared war on typography and orthography as well. And
finally we return to the narrative of St. Luke, whose
simplicity of language reinforces the austerity of the story of
how Christmas began.

Bonnie Dudley Edwards suggested the idea of this book,
and helped with its creation. The Rev. Marcus Lefebure,
O.P., placed at our disposal the programmes of readings he
has directed for many years at the Catholic Chaplaincy of
Edinburgh University. We are also grateful to: the Estate of
P. G. Wodehouse and Hutchinson Publishing Group Ltd. for
"Sundered Hearts" from *The Clicking of Cuthbert*; the Estate
of G. K. Chesterton and Cassell Ltd. for "The Flying Stars"
from *The Innocence of Father Brown*; the National Trust and
Eyre Methuen Ltd. for "Christmas in India" from *The
Definitive Edition of Rudyard Kipling's Verse*; the Estate of
Christopher Murray Grieve for "The Innumerable Christ"
from *The Complete Poems of Hugh MacDiarmid*; Anthony Ross,
Conor Cruise O'Brien, Alan Boyd, Michael Horniman,
Allen Wright, Ian Boyd, Elizabeth Balbirnie Lee, Michael
Grieve, Richard Lancelyn Green, Timothy Willis,
Rosemary Gentleman, Sile Ni Shúilleabháin, Nicolas

Barker, Iain Lindsay Smith, the National Library of
Scotland, Edinburgh University Library, the British
Museum.

"A Christmas Letter" is here reprinted with permission of
The Bodley Head from *Literary Lapses* by Stephen Leacock.

EDINBURGH UNIVERSITY STUDENT   *Owen Dudley Edwards*
PUBLICATIONS BOARD   *Graham Richardson*

John Milton

ON THE MORNING OF
CHRISTS NATIVITY

I

THIS is the Month, and this the happy morn
Wherin the Son of Heav'ns eternal King,
Of wedded Maid, and Virgin Mother born,
Our great redemption from above did bring;
For so the holy sages once did sing,
   That he our deadly forfeit should release,
And with his Father work us a perpetual peace.

II

That glorious Form, that Light unsufferable,
And that far-beaming blaze of Majesty,
Wherwith he wont at Heav'ns high Councel-Table,
To sit the midst of Trinal Unity,
He laid aside; and here with us to be,
   Forsook the Courts of everlasting Day,
And chose with us a darksom House of mortal Clay.

III

Say Heav'nly Muse, shall not thy sacred vein
Afford a present to the Infant God?

Hast thou no vers, no hymn, or solemn strein,
To welcom him to this his new abode,
Now while the Heav'n by the Suns team untrod,
    Hath took no print of the approching light,
And all the spangled host keep watch in squadrons bright?

IV

See how far upon the Eastern rode
The Star-led Wisards haste with odours sweet:
O run, prevent them with thy humble ode,
And lay it lowly at his blessed feet;
Have thou the honour first, thy Lord to greet,
    And joyn thy voice unto the Angel Quire,
From out his secret Altar toucht with hallow'd fire.

THE HYMN

I

IT was the Winter wilde,
  While the Heav'n-born-childe,
    All meanly wrapt in the rude manger lies;
Nature in aw to him
Had doff't her gawdy trim,
    With her great Master so to sympathize:
It was no season then for her
To wanton with the Sun her lusty Paramour.

II

Onely with speeches fair
She woo's the gentle Air
    To hide her guilty front with innocent Snow;

And on her naked shame,
Pollute with sinfull blame,
   The Saintly Vail of Maiden white to throw,
Confounded, that her Makers eyes
Should look so neer upon her foul deformities.

III

But he her fears to cease,
Sent down the meek-eyd Peace,
   She crown'd with Olive green, came softly sliding
Down through the turning sphear
His ready Harbinger,
   With Turtle wing the amorous clouds dividing,
And waving wide her mirtle wand,
She strikes a universall Peace through Sea and Land.

IV

No War, or Battails sound
Was heard the World around:
   The idle spear and shield were high up hung;
The hooked Chariot stood
Unstain'd with hostile blood,
   The Trumpet spake not to the armed throng,
And Kings sate still with awfull eye,
As if they surely knew their sovran Lord was by.

V

But peacefull was the night
Wherin the Prince of light
   His raign of peace upon the earth began:
The Windes with wonder whist,
Smoothly the waters kist,
   Whispering new joyes to the milde Ocean,
Who now hath quite forgot to rave,
While Birds of Calm sit brooding on the charmed wave.

VI

The Stars with deep amaze
Stand fixt in stedfast gaze,
   Bending one way their pretious influence,
And will not take their flight,
For all the morning light,
   Or *Lucifer* that often warn'd them thence;
But in their glimmering Orbs did glow,
Until their Lord himself bespake, and bid them go.

VII

And though the shady gloom
Had given day her room,
   The Sun himself with-held his wonted speed,
And hid his head for shame,
As his inferiour flame,
   The new-enlightn'd world no more should need;
He saw a greater Sun appear
Then his bright Throne, or burning Axletree could bear.

VIII

The Shepherds on the Lawn,
Or ere the point of dawn,
   Sate simply chatting in a rustick row;
Full little thought they than,
That the mighty *Pan*
   Was kindly com to live with them below;
Perhaps their loves, or els their sheep,
Was all that did their silly thoughts so busie keep.

IX

When such musick sweet
Their hearts and ears did greet,
   As never was by mortall finger strook,
Divinely-warbled voice

Answering the stringed noise,
  As all their souls in blisfull rapture took:
The Air such pleasure loth to lose,
With thousand echo's still prolongs each heav'nly close.

X

Nature that heard such sound
Beneath the hollow round
  Of *Cynthia*'s seat, the Airy region thrilling.
Now was almost won
To think her part was don,
  And that her raign had here its last fulfilling;
She knew such harmony alone
Could hold all Heav'n and Earth in happier union.

XI

At last surrounds their sight
A Globe of circular light,
  That with long beams the shame-fac't night array'd,
The helmed Cherubim
And sworded Seraphim,
  Are seen in glittering ranks with wings displaid,
Harping in loud and solemn quire,
With unexpressive notes to Heav'ns new-born Heir.

XII

Such Musick (as 'tis said)
Before was never made,
  But when of old the sons of morning sung,
While the Creator Great
His constellations set,
  And the well-ballanc't world on hinges hung,
And cast the dark foundations deep,
And bid the weltring waves their oozy channel keep.

XIII

Ring out ye Crystall sphears,
Once bless our human ears,
  (If ye have power to touch our senses so)
And let your silver chime
Move in melodious time;
  And let the Base of Heav'ns deep Organ blow,
And with your ninefold harmony
Make up full consort to th'Angelike symphony.

XIV

For if such holy Song
Enwrap our fancy long,
  Time will run back, and fetch the age of gold,
And speckl'd vanity
Will sicken soon and die,
  And leprous sin will melt from earthly mould,
And Hell it self will pass away,
And leave her dolorous mansions to the peering day.

XV

Yea Truth, and Justice then
Will down return to men,
  Orb'd in a Rain-bow; and like glories wearing
Mercy will sit between,
Thron'd in Celestiall sheen,
  With radiant feet the tissued clouds down stearing,
And Heav'n as at som festivall,
Will open wide the gates of her high Palace Hall.

XVI

But wisest Fate sayes no,
This must not yet be so,
  The Babe lies yet in smiling Infancy,
That on the bitter cross

Must redeem our loss;
  So both himself and us to glorifie:
Yet first to those ychain'd in sleep,
The wakefull trump of doom must thunder through the deep,

XVII

With such a horrid clang
As on mount *Sinai* rang
  While the red fire, and smouldring clouds out brake:
The aged Earth agast
With terrour of that blast,
  Shall from the surface to the center shake;
When at the worlds last session,
The dreadfull Judge in middle Air shall spread his throne.

XVIII

And then at last our bliss
Full and perfect is,
  But now begins; for from this happy day
Th'old Dragon under ground
In straiter limits bound,
  Not half so far casts his usurped sway,
And wrath to see his Kingdom fail,
Swindges the scaly Horrour of his foulded tail.

XIX

The Oracles are dumm,
No voice or hideous humm
  Runs through the arched roof in words deceiving.
Apollo from his shrine
Can no more divine,
  With hollow shreik the steep of *Delphos* leaving.
No nightly trance, or breathed spell,
Inspire's the pale-ey'd Priest from the prophetic cell.

XX

The lonely mountains o're,
And the resounding shore,
    A voice of weeping heard, and loud lament;
From haunted spring, and dale
Edg'd with poplar pale.
    The parting Genius is with sighing sent,
With flowre-inwov'n tresses torn
The Nimphs in twilight shade of tangled thickets mourn.

XXI

In consecrated Earth,
And on the holy Hearth,
    The *Lars*, and *Lemures* moan with midnight plaint,
In Urns, and Altars round,
A drear, and dying sound
    Affrights the *Flamins* at their service quaint;
And the chill Marble seems to sweat,
While each peculiar power forgoes his wonted seat.

XXII

Peor, and *Baalim*,
Forsake their Temples dim,
    With that twise batter'd god of *Palestine*,
And mooned *Ashtaroth*,
Heav'ns Queen and Mother both,
    Now sits not girt with Tapers holy shine,
The Libyc *Hammon* shrinks his horn,
In vain the *Tyrian* Maids their wounded *Thamuz* mourn.

XXIII

And sullen *Moloch* fled,
Hath left in shadows dred,
    His burning Idol all of blackest hue,
In vain with Cymbals ring.

They call the grisly king,
   In dismall dance about the furnace blue,
The brutish gods of *Nile* as fast,
Isis and *Orus*, and the Dog *Anubis* hast.

XXIV

Nor is *Osiris* seen
In *Memphian* Grove, or Green,
   Trampling the unshowr'd Grasse with lowings loud:
Nor can he be at rest
Within his sacred chest,
   Naught but profoundest Hell can be his shroud,
In vain with Timbrel'd Anthems dark
The sable-stoled Sorcerers bear his worshipt Ark.

XXV

He feels from *Juda*'s Land
The dredded Infants hand,
   The rayes of *Bethlehem* blind his dusky eyn;
Nor all the gods beside,
Longer dare abide,
   Not *Typhon* huge ending in snaky twine:
Our Babe to shew his Godhead true,
Can in his swaddling bands controul the damned crew.

XXVI

So when the Sun in bed,
Curtain'd with cloudy red,
   Pillows his chin upon an Orient wave.
The flocking shadows pale,
Troop to th'infernall jail,
   Each fetter'd Ghost slips to his severall grave,
And the yellow-skirted *Fayes*,
Fly after the Night-steeds, leaving their Moon-lov'd maze.

XXVII

But see the Virgin blest,
Hath laid her Babe to rest.
   Time is our tedious song should here have ending;
Heavn's youngest-teemed star
Hath fixed her polished car,
   Her sleeping Lord with handmaid lamp attending;
And all about the courtly stable
Bright-harnessed angels sit in order serviceable.

CHRISTMAS CAROL

THE narrator said: On the Night of the Gifts the good-wives used to put the bannock-stone into the laps of their girl-children — as a symbol of Brigit, since she was the first woman who took Christ the Son of God into her lap. There is a dear hymn concerning this, but I do not remember it. I have lost my memory since I lost my means and since my people were scattered — some of them in Australia, and some of them in Canada, and some of them mouldering in the dust. Oh the turns of the hard world! Many a trick does it play, and so it was with me. My fresh new house was burned over my head, and I burned my hands in rescuing my dear little children. Oh the suffering of the poor folk! The terrible time that was! The land was taken from us, though we were not a penny in debt, and all the lands of the townland were given to the Lowland farmer beside us. He had always been wishing to have them, and he never stopped until he got them.

The night is the long night,
   Hù ri vì hó hù,
It will snow and it will drift,
   Hù ri vì hó hù,
White snow there will be till day,
   Hù ri vì hó hù,
White moon there will be till morn,
   Hù ri vì hó hù.

This night is the eve of the Great Nativity,
   Hù ri vì hó hù,
This night is born Mary Virgin's Son,
   Hù ri vì hó hù,
This night is born Jesus, Song of the King of glory,
   Hù ri vì hó hù,
This night is born to us the root of our joy,
   Hù ri vì hó hù,
This night gleamed the sun of the mountains high,
   Hù ri vì hó hù,
This night gleamed sea and shore together,
   Hù ri vì hó hù,
This night was born Christ the King of greatness,
   Hù ri vì hó hù.
Ere it was heard that the Glory was come,
   Hù ri vì hó hù,
Heard was the wave upon the strand,
   Hù ri vì hó hù;
Ere 'twas heard that His foot had reached the earth,
   Hù ri vì hó hù,
Heard was the song of the angels glorious,
   Hù ri vì hó hù.
This night is the long night,
   Hù ri vì hó hù.

Glowed to Him wood and tree,
   Glowed to Him mount and sea,
Glowed to Him land and plain,
   When that His foot was come to earth.

Traditonal

ANE SANG OF THE BIRTH OF CHRIST

I COME from heuin to tell
 The best nowellis that euer befell,
To zow thir tythingis trew I bring,
And I will of them say and sing.

This day, to zow, is borne ane childe
Of Marie meik, and Virgin milde.
That blissit bairne bening and kynde,
Sall zow reioyis, baith hart and mynde.

It is the Lord, Christ, God and Man,
He will do for zow quhat he can:
Him self zour Sauiour will be,
Fra sin and hell, to mak zow fré.

He is zour rycht Saluatioun,
From euerlasting Dampnatioun:
That ze may Ring in gloir and blis,
For euer mair in heuin with his.

Ze sall him find, but mark or wying,
Full sempill in ane Cribe lying:
Sa lyis he quhilk zow hes wrocht,
And all this warld maid of nocht.

Lat vs reioyis and be blyith,
And with the Hyrdis go full swyith,
And sé quhat God of his grace hes done,
Throw Christ to bring vs to his throne.

My Saull and lyfe stand up and sé
Quha lyis in ane Cribbe of tré:
Quhat Babe is that, sa gude and fair?
It is Christ, Goddis Sone and air.

Welcome now, gracious God of mycht,
To sinnaris vyle, pure and vnrycht.
Thow come to saif vs from distres,
How can we thank thy gentilnes!

O God that maid all Creature,
How art thow now becumit sa pure,
That on the hay and stray will ly,
Amang the Assis, Oxin and Ky?

And war the warld ten tymes sa wyde,
Cled ouer with gold, and stanis of pryde,
Unworthie it war, zit to thé,
Under thy feit ane stule to be.

The Sylk and Sandell thé to eis,
Ar hay, and sempill sweilling clais,
Quharin thow gloris greitest King,
As thow in heuin war in thy Ring.

Thow tuke sic panis temporall,
To mak me ryche perpetuall.
For all this warldis welth and gude,
Can na thing ryche they celsitude.

O my deir hart, zung Jesus sweit,
Prepair thy creddill in my Spreit,
And I sall rock thé in my hart,
And neuer mair fra thé depart.

Bot I sall pryse thé euer moir,
With sangis sweit vnto thy gloir:
The kneis of my hart sall I bow,
And sing that rycht Balulalow.

Gloir be to God Eternallie,
Quhilk gaif his onlie Sone for me:
The angellis Joyis for to heir,
The gracious gift of this new Zeir.

Anon.

PREPARATIONS

YET if His Majesty, our sovran lord,
   Should of his own accord
Friendly himself invite,
And say "I'll be your guest to-morrow night,"
How should we stir ourselves, call and command
All hands to work. "Let no man idle stand!

"Set me fine Spanish tables in the hall;
See they be fitted all;
Let there be room to eat
And order taken that there want no meat.
See every sconce and candlestick made bright,
That without tapers they may give a light.

"Look to the presence: are the carpets spread,
The dazie o'er the head,
The cushions in the chairs,
And all the candles lighted on the stairs?
Perfume the chambers, and in any case
Let each man give attendance in his place."

Thus, if a king were coming, would we do;
And 'twere good reason too;

For 'tis a duteous thing
To show all honour to an earthly king,
And after all our travail and our cost,
So he be pleased, to think no labour lost.

But at the coming of the King of Heaven
All's set at six and seven;
We wallow in our sin,
Christ cannot find a chamber in the inn.
We entertain Him always like a stranger,
And, as at first, still lodge Him in the manger.

John Donne

NATIVITIE

IMMENSITIE cloysterd in thy deare wombe,
  Now leaves his welbelov'd imprisonment,
There he hath made himselfe to his intent
Weake enough, now into our world to come;
But Oh, for thee, for him, hath th'Inne no roome?
Yet lay him in this stall, and from the Orient,
Starres, and wisemen will travell to prevent
Th'effect of *Herods* jealous generall doome.
Seest thou, my Soule, with thy faiths eyes, how he
Which fils all place, yet none holds him, doth lye?
Was not his pity towards thee wondrous high,
That would have need to be pittied by thee?
Kisse him, and with him into Egypt goe,
With his kinde mother, who partakes thy woe.

Hugh MacDiarmid

THE INNUMERABLE CHRIST

Other stars may have their Bethlehem, and their
Calvary too. —Professor J. Y. SIMPSON

WHA kens on whatna Bethlehems
Earth twinkles like a star the nicht,
An' whatna shepherds lift their heids
In its unearthly licht?

'Yont a' the stars oor een can see
An' farther than their lichts can fly,
I' mony an unco warl' the nicht
The fatefu' bairnies cry.

I' mony an unco warl' the nicht
The lift gaes black as pitch at noon,
An' sideways on their chests the heids
O' endless Christs roll doon.

An' when the earth's as cauld's the mune
An' a' its folk are lang syne deid,
On coontless stars the Babe maun cry
An' the Crucified maun bleed.

Anthony Ross

CHRIST RAN STUMBLING

CHRIST ran stumbling down the street
    on little twisted feet;
small blue hands over the place
where someone had bruised his face.
His starved, thin body shook with tears
and quick short gasps of fear.

Bitter the December day,
streets and sky an equal gray;
no brightness, but the neoned pub
where city men with Christmas grin
forgetfully went out and in.

When did we see you? folk will say,
at the last day.

Conor Cruise O'Brien

LONG DAY'S JOURNEY INTO PRAYER

JUST before last Christmas it so happened that I wanted to say a prayer. I stifled the temptation.

It came back, as temptations do. I found myself engaged in the following internal dialogue:—

"So you want to say a prayer? Why don't you get on with it, and stop annoying me?"

"I won't get on with it because I'm an agnostic."

"What's that got to do with it?"

"An agnostic is someone who doesn't believe in God."

"So what?"

"You can't say a prayer to someone you don't believe in."

"Why can't you?"

"Um."

My father had been an agnostic. We lived in Dublin. Agnosticism ran in the family, a bit: my mother's eldest sister and her son Owen were agnostics, too. All the rest were Catholics, traditional, Tridentine. My mother had tried being an agnostic, out of loyalty to my father. When he died she gave up and went back to being a Catholic. She also started to pray hard, very hard, even for an Irish Roman Catholic. She started praying on Christmas Night 1927. The reason why she started praying on that particular night was that my father died that morning, suddenly, of a heart attack, while bending a bow for me, my present from him.

You can forget about the bow. The important word, as any Roman Catholic reader sees instantly, is "suddenly".

There was no time to send for the priest. If there had been, my mother would most certainly have asked my father to send for him. And I believe he *would* have sent for him, mainly because he knew it would be a comfort to my mother and — therefore — to me. For the same sort of reason, James Joyce, another Dublin Catholic agnostic, but of much stricter obedience than my father, felt able to tell his little sister that their mother was in Heaven.

Being a *live* agnostic was not then — and is not now — taken very seriously in Ireland. Not very long ago a prominent Belfast Catholic revealed to his Parish Priest that he (the PBC) had become an agnostic. The man of God kept his cool: "You're not an agnostic, Paddy. You're just a fat slob who's too lazy to go to Mass."

But to be an agnostic *who had died without the priest* was, in 1927, and for years afterwards, a much more serious matter. Everybody we knew well was kind to my mother about this. They explained to my mother that my father would certainly go to Heaven, because he had "lived a good life". These reassurances were in themselves alarming. What my mother was worried about was not *whether* my father would go to Heaven — she took that for granted — but *when* he would get there.

The great question, in fact, was Purgatory, a thriving institution at the time. My mother did not believe — as a less educated widow in her position might have believed, and would have been *told* — that her husband was undergoing a course of physical torture somewhere under the earth. She believed that he might be "separated from God". It was not the separation from God that worried her: it was the separation from *her*. By her bedside I saw for the first time, in early January 1928, a manual of devotion: *In Heaven We Know Our Own* by Fr. Blot, S.J. I didn't need to read the book. The title was enough.

You see, to know your own in Heaven, your own have to get there, and I knew that the date of my father's arrival at that destination was problematical. The reason for that was myself. Because my father, besides being an agnostic, and dying without the priest, had done something much worse: he had sent me to a Protestant school, because he thought Protestant schools were better than Catholic ones, which they were.

My mother was told that if she prayed she could *shorten* my father's term in purgatory. So she prayed like mad. But she was also told that every term she kept me on at a Protestant school *lengthened* my father's term of suffering. She would not take me away from that school because it had been my father's wish that I should go there, and that was that. Every day of her life was shortening, lengthening, praying and holding firm, with heroic fortitude.

Years afterwards, a Pope decided that enough was enough, and closed Purgatory down. Of course, he said he *wasn't* closing the place down, it had just somehow never been there. It had been there all right, I knew, because my mother was shut up in it for more than ten years, from Christmas 1927 to her death at Easter 1938.

These transactions left me, naturally, with a dislike of the God about whose character, methods and punitive accountancy so much curious and precise information had been so pressingly conveyed to my mother. Dislike took the form of disbelief. The transition was very neatly expressed by my cousin, Owen — older and tougher and wittier than I — who, being asked by a clergyman why he considered that God didn't exist, made the gentle, wide-eyed answer: "Don't you think it's the most charitable hypothesis?"

That was the stuff to give them.

I was left with two other things: a kind of shiver recurring every Christmas Day, and a horror of prayer. The prayers I had been closest to were the cries of pain wrung from my mother by her spiritual tormentors. Think anyone was going to get one of *those* out of me? Not a prayer! But somebody did.

After a car accident, on 14 November last year, my wife was seriously ill in Jervis Street Hospital, Dublin. That hospital must be one of the best in the world; in the quality of its medical care and of its nursing and in constant personal kindness. It is run by nuns.

My wife is a practising Catholic. She asked people — not me — to pray for her, and they did. People asked me to tell her they were praying for her, and I did. People came up to me in the street and asked how she was. When I told them things were not so good, they said please God. When I told them things were getting better, they said thank God, and that a lot of people had been praying for her.

In the street conversations I did not re-echo the please God. But when it came to thanking God, I found myself repeating it all right. I felt a bit guilty about this, but, after all, they were decent people and it was only civil.

Things began to move from please God to thank God just before Christmas. On Christmas Day we knew for sure she was going to be all right. I brought in the children. We shared champagne and Coke with the nurses. Thank God spanged out on all sides. I joined in recklessly, not out of civility, but out of sheer joy. She was going to be all right. Thank God.

It didn't matter a damn whether I believed in God or not, or even whether I *wanted* to thank Him. I was just thanking Him anyway: and I noticed something.

The old shiver, inseparable from every Christmas Day over exactly half a century, had clean gone. I had often read "The Ancient Mariner", but that Christmas morning in St. Agnes Ward, I *was* that venerable seafarer. That damned bird had gone! There was nothing round my neck anymore!

The self-same moment I could pray.

G. K. Chesterton

THE FLYING STARS

"THE most beautiful crime I ever committed," Flambeau would say in his highly moral old age, "was also, by a singular coincidence, my last. It was committed at Christmas. As an artist I had always attempted to provide crimes suitable to the special season or landscapes in which I found myself, choosing this or that terrace or garden for a catastrophe, as if for a statuary group. Thus squires should be swindled in long rooms panelled with oak; while Jews, on the other hand, should rather find themselves unexpectedly penniless among the light and screens of the Café Riche. Thus, in England, if I wished to relieve a dean of his riches (which is not so easy as you might suppose), I wished to frame him, if I make myself clear, in the green lawns and grey towers of some cathedral town. Similarly, in France, when I had got money out of a rich and wicked peasant (which is almost impossible), it gratified me to get his indignant head relieved against a grey line of clipped poplars, and those solemn plains of Gaul over which broods the mighty spirit of Millet.

"Well, my last crime was a Christmas crime, a cheery, cosy, English middle-class crime; a crime of Charles Dickens. I did it in a good old middle-class house near Putney, a house with a crescent of carriage drive, a house with a stable by the side of it, a house with the name on the two outer gates, a house with a monkey tree. Enough, you know the species. I really think my imitation of Dickens's style was dexterous and literary. It seems almost a pity I repented the same evening."

Flambeau would then proceed to tell the story from the inside; and even from the inside it was odd. Seen from the outside it was perfectly incomprehensible, and it is from the outside that the stranger must study it. From this standpoint the drama may be said to have begun when the front doors of the house with the stable opened on the garden with the monkey tree, and a young girl came out with bread to feed the birds on the afternoon of Boxing Day. She had a pretty face, with brave brown eyes; but her figure was beyond conjecture, for she was so wrapped up in brown furs that it was hard to say which was hair and which was fur. But for the attractive face she might have been a small toddling bear.

The winter afternoon was reddening towards evening, and already a ruby light was rolled over the bloomless beds, filling them, as it were, with the ghosts of the dead roses. On the one side of the house stood the stable, on the other an alley or cloister of laurels led to the larger garden behind. The young lady, having scattered bread for the birds (for the fourth or fifth time that day, because the dog ate it), passed unobtrusively down the lane of laurels and into a glimmering plantation of evergreen behind. Here she gave an exclamation of wonder, real or ritual, and looking up at the high garden wall above her, beheld it fantastically bestridden by a somewhat fantastic figure.

"Oh, don't jump, Mr Crook," she called out in some alarm; "it's much too high."

The individual riding the party wall like an aerial horse was a tall, angular young man, with dark hair sticking up like a hair brush, intelligent and even distinguished lineaments, but a sallow and almost alien complexion. This showed the more plainly because he wore an aggressive red tie, the only part of his costume of which he seemed to take any care. Perhaps it was a symbol. He took no notice of the girl's alarmed adjuration, but leapt like a grasshopper to the ground beside her, where he might very well have broken his legs.

"I think I was meant to be a burglar," he said placidly, "and I have no doubt I should have been if I hadn't happened to be born in that nice house next door. I can't see any harm in it, anyhow."

"How can you say such things?" she remonstrated.

"Well," said the young man, "if you're born on the wrong side of the wall, I can't see that it's wrong to climb over."

"I never know what you will say or do next," she said.

"I don't often know myself," replied Mr Crook; "but then I am on the right side of the wall now."

"And which is the right side of the wall?" asked the young lady, smiling.

"Whichever side you are on," said the young man named Crook.

As they went together through the laurels towards the front garden a motor horn sounded thrice, coming nearer and nearer, and a car of splendid speed, great elegance, and a pale green colour swept up to the front doors like a bird and stood throbbing.

"Hullo, hullo!" said the young man with the red tie; "here's somebody born on the right side, anyhow. I didn't know, Miss Adams, that your Santa Claus was so modern as this."

"Oh, that's my godfather, Sir Leopold Fischer. He always comes on Boxing Day."

Then, after an innocent pause, which unconsciously betrayed some lack of enthusiasm, Ruby Adams added: "He is very kind."

John Crook, journalist, had heard of that eminent City magnate; and it was not his fault if the City magnate had not heard of him; for in certain articles in *The Clarion* or *The New Age* Sir Leopold had been dealt with austerely. But he said nothing and grimly watched the unloading of the motor car, which was rather a long process. A large, neat chauffeur in green got out from the front, and a small, neat manservant in grey got out from the back, and between them they deposited Sir Leopold on the doorstep and began to unpack him, like some very carefully protected parcel. Rugs enough to stock a bazaar, furs of all the beasts of the forest, and scarves of all the colours of the rainbow were unwrapped one by one, till they revealed something resembling the human form; the form of a friendly, but foreign-looking old gentleman, with a grey goat-like beard and a beaming smile, who rubbed his big fur gloves together.

Long before this revelation was complete the two big doors of the porch had opened in the middle, and Colonel Adams (father of the furry young lady) had come out himself to invite his eminent guest inside. He was a tall, sunburnt and very silent man, who wore a red smoking-cap like a fez, making him look like one of the English Sirdars or Pashas in Egypt. With him was his brother-in-law, lately come from Canada, a big and rather boisterous young gentleman-farmer, with a yellow beard, by name James Blount. With him also was the more insignificant figure of the priest from the neighbouring Roman church; for the colonel's late wife had been a Catholic, and the children, as is common in such cases, had been trained to follow her. Everything seemed undistinguished about the priest, even down to his name, which was Brown; yet the colonel had always found something companionable about him, and frequently asked him to such family gatherings.

In the large entrance hall of the house there was ample room even for Sir Leopold and the removel of his wraps. Porch and vestibule, indeed, were unduly large in proportion to the house, and formed, as it were, a big room with the front door at one end, and the bottom of the staircase at the other. In front of the large hall fire, over which hung the colonel's sword, the process was completed and the company, including the saturnine Crook, presented to Sir Leopold Fischer. That venerable financier, however, still seemed struggling with portions of his well-lined attire, and at length produced from a very interior tail-coat pocket, a black oval case which he radiantly explained to be his Christmas present for his god-daughter. With an unaffected vainglory that had something disarming about it he held out the case before them all; it flew open at a touch and half-blinded them. It was just as if a crystal fountain had spurted in their eyes. In a nest of orange velvet lay like three eggs, three white and vivid diamonds that seemed to set the very air on fire all round them. Fischer stood beaming benevolently and drinking deep of the astonishment and ecstasy of the girl, the grim admiration and gruff thanks of the colonel, the wonder of the whole group.

"I'll put 'em back now, my dear," said Fischer, returning the case to the tails of his coat. "I had to be careful of 'em coming down. They're the three great African diamonds called 'The Flying Stars', because they've been stolen so often. All the big criminals are on the track; but even the rough men about in the streets and hotels could hardly have kept their hands off them. I might have lost them on the road here. It was quite possible."

"Quite natural, I should say," growled the man in the red tie. "I shouldn't blame 'em if they had taken 'em. When they ask for bread, and you don't even give them a stone, I think they might take the stone for themselves."

"I won't have you talking like that," cried the girl, who was in a curious glow. "You've only talked like that since you became a horrid what's-his-name. You know what I mean. What do you call a man who wants to embrace the chimney-sweep?"

"A saint," said Father Brown.

"I think," said Sir Leopold, with a supercilious smile, "that Ruby means a Socialist."

"A Radical does not mean a man who lives on radishes," remarked Crook, with some impatience; "and a

Conservative does not mean a man who preserves jam. Neither, I assure you, does a Socialist mean a man who desires a social evening with the chimney-sweep. A Socialist means a man who wants all the chimneys swept and all the chimney-sweeps paid for it."

"But who won't allow you," put in the priest in a low voice, "to own your own soot."

Crook looked at him with an eye of interest and even respect. "Does one want to own soot?" he asked.

"One might," answered Brown, with speculation in his eye. "I've heard that gardeners use it. And I once made six children happy at Christmas when the conjurer didn't come, entirely with soot — applied externally."

"Oh, splendid," cried Ruby. "Oh, I wish you'd do it to this company."

The boisterous Canadian, Mr Blount, was lifting his loud voice in applause, and the astonished financier his (in some considerable deprecation), when a knock sounded at the double front doors. The priest opened them, and they showed again the front garden of evergreens, monkey-tree and all, now gathering gloom against a gorgeous violet sunset. The scene thus framed was so coloured and quaint, like a back scene in a play, that they forgot for a moment the insignificant figure standing in the door. He was dusty-looking and in a frayed coat, evidently a common messenger. "Any of you gentlemen Mr Blount?" he asked, and held forward a letter doubtfully. Mr Blount started, and stopped in his shout of assent. Ripping up the envelope with evident astonishment, he read it; his face clouded a little, and then cleared, and he turned to his brother-in-law and host.

"I'm sick at being such a nuisance, colonel," he said, with the cheery colonial convention; "but would it upset you if an old acquaintance called on me here tonight on business? In point of fact it's Florian, that famous French acrobat and comic actor; I knew him years ago out West (he was a

French-Canadian by birth), and he seems to have business for me, though I hardly guess what."

"Of course, of course," replied the colonel carelessly. "My dear chap, any friend of yours. No doubt he will prove an acquisition."

"He'll black his face, if that's what you mean," cried Blount, laughing. "I don't doubt he'd black everyone else's eyes. I don't care; I'm not refined. I like the jolly old pantomime where a man sits on his top hat."

"Not on mine, please," said Sir Leopold Fischer, with dignity.

"Well, well," observed Crook airily, "don't let's quarrel. There are lower jokes than sitting on a top hat."

Dislike of the red-tied youth, both of his predatory opinions and evident intimacy with the pretty god-child, led Fischer to say, in his most sarcastic, magisterial manner: "No doubt you have found something much lower than sitting on a top hat. What is it, pray?"

"Letting a top hat sit on you, for instance," said the Socialist.

"Now, now, now," cried the Canadian farmer with his barbarian benevolence, "don't let's spoil a jolly evening. What I say is, let's do something for the company tonight. Not blacking faces or sitting on hats, if you don't like those — but something of the sort. Why couldn't we have a proper old English pantomime — clown, columbine, and so on. I saw one when I left England at twelve years old, and it's blazed in my brain like a bonfire ever since. I came back to the old country only last year, and I find the thing's extinct. Nothing but a lot of snivelling fairy plays. I want a hot poker and a policeman made into sausages, and they give me princesses moralising by moonlight, Blue Birds, or something. Blue Beard's more in my line, and him I liked best when he turned into the pantaloon."

"I'm all for making a policeman into sausages," said John Crook. "It's a better definition of Socialism than some recently given. But surely the get-up would be too big a business."

"Not a scrap," cried Blount, quite carried away. "A harlequinade's the quickest thing we can do, for two reasons. First, one can gag to any degree; and, second, all the objects are household things — tables and towel-horses and washing baskets, and things like that."

"That's true," admitted Crook, nodding eagerly and walking about. "But I'm afraid I can't have my policeman's uniform! Haven't killed a policeman lately."

Blount frowned thoughtfully a space, and then smote his thigh. "Yes, we can!" he cried. "I've got Florian's address here, and he knows every *costumier* in London. I'll phone him to bring a police dress when he comes." And he went bounding away to the telephone.

"Oh, it's glorious, godfather," cried Ruby, almost dancing. "I'll be columbine and you shall be pantaloon."

The millionaire held himself stiff with a sort of heathen solemnity. "I think, my dear," he said, "you must get someone else for pantaloon."

"I will be pantaloon, if you like," said Colonel Adams, taking his cigar out of his mouth, and speaking for the first and last time.

"You ought to have a statue," cried the Canadian, as he came back, radiant, from the telephone. "There, we are all fitted. Mr Crook shall be clown; he's a journalist and knows all the oldest jokes. I can be harlequin, that only wants long legs and jumping about. My friend Florian 'phones he's bringing the police costume, he's changing on the way. We can act it in this very hall, the audience sitting on those broad stairs opposite, one row above another. These front doors can be the back scene, either open or shut. Shut, you seen an English interior. Open, a moonlit garden. It all goes by magic." And snatching a chance piece of billiard chalk from his pocket, he ran it across the hall floor, halfway between the front door and the staircase, to mark the line of the footlights.

How even such a banquet of bosh was got ready in the time remained a riddle. But they went at it with that mixture of recklessness and industry that lives when youth is in a house; and youth was in that house that night, though not all may have isolated the two faces and hearts from which it flamed. As always happens, the invention grew wilder and wilder through the very tameness of the *bourgeois* conventions from which it had to create. The columbine looked charming in an outstanding skirt that strangely resembled the large lampshade in the drawing-room. The clown and pantaloon made themselves white with flour from the cook, and red with rouge from some other domestic, who remained (like all true Christian benefactors) anonymous. The harlequin, already clad in silver paper out of cigar boxes, was, with difficulty, prevented from smashing the old Victorian lustre chandeliers, that he might cover himself with resplendent crystals. In fact he would certainly have done so, had not Ruby unearthed some old pantomime paste jewels she had worn at a fancy-dress party as the Queen of Diamonds. Indeed, her uncle, James Blount, was getting almost out of hand in his excitement; he was like a schoolboy. He put a paper donkey's head unexpectedly on Father Brown, who bore it patiently, and even found some private manner of moving his ears. He even essayed to put the paper donkey's tail to the coat-tails of Sir Leopold Fischer. This, however, was frowned down. "Uncle is too absurd," cried Ruby to Crook, round whose shoulders she had seriously place a string of sausages. "Why is he so wild?"

"He is harlequin to your columbine," said Crook. "I am only the clown who makes the old jokes."

"I wish you were the harlequin," she said, and left the string of sausages swinging.

Father Brown, though he knew every detail done behind the scenes, and had even evoked applause by his transforma-

tion of a pillow into a pantomime baby, went round to the
front and sat among the audience with all the solemn
expectation of a child at his first matinée. The spectators
were few, relations, one or two local friends, and the
servants; Sir Leopold sat in the front seat, his full and still
fur-collared figure largely obscuring the view of the little
cleric behind him; but it has never been settled by artistic
authorities whether the cleric lost much. The pantomime
was utterly chaotic, yet not contemptible; there ran through
it a rage of improvisation which came chiefly from Crook
the clown. Commonly he was a clever man, and he was
inspired tonight with a wild omniscience, a folly wiser than
the world, that which comes to a young man who has seen
for an instant a particular expression on a particular face. He
was supposed to be the clown, but he was really almost
everything else, the author (so far as there was an author),
the prompter, the scene-painter, the scene-shifter, and,
above all, the orchestra. At abrupt intervals in the
outrageous performance he would hurl himself in full
costume at the piano and bang out some popular music
equally absurd and appropriate.

The climax of this, as of all else, was the moment when the
two front doors at the back of the scene flew open, showing
the lovely moonlit garden, but showing more prominently
the famous professional guest; the great Florian, dressed up
as a policeman. The clown at the piano played the
constabulary chorus in the *Pirates of Penzance*, but it was
drowned in the deafening applause, for every gesture of the
great comic actor was an admirable though restrained
version of the carriage and manner of the police. The
harlequin leapt upon him and hit him over the helmet; the
pianist playing "Where did you get that hat?" he faced about
in admirably simulated astonishment, and then the leaping
harlequin hit him again (the pianist suggesting a few bars of
"Then we had another one"). Then the harlequin rushed
right into the arms of the policeman and fell on top of him,

amid a roar of applause. Then it was that the strange actor gave that celebrated imitation of a dead man, of which the fame still lingers around Putney. It was almost impossible to believe a living person could appear so limp.

The athletic harlequin swung him about like a sack or twisted or tossed him like an Indian club; all the time to the most maddeningly ludicrous tunes from the piano. When the harlequin heaved the comic constable heavily off the floor the clown played "I arise from dreams of thee". When he shuffled him across his back, "With my bundle on my shoulder", and when the harlequin finally let fall the policeman with a most convincing thud, the lunatic at the instrument stuck into a jingling measure with some words which are still believed to have been "I sent a letter to my love and on the way I dropped it".

At about this limit of mental anarchy Father Brown's view was obscured altogether; for the City magnate in front of him rose to his full height and thrust his hands savagely into all his pockets. Then he sat down nervously, still fumbling, and then stood up again. For an instant it seemed seriously likely that he would stride across the footlights; then he turned a glare at the clown playing the piano; and then he burst in silence out of the room.

The priest had only watched for a few more minutes the absurd but not inelegant dance of the amateur harlequin over his splendidly unconscious foe. With real though rude art, the harlequin danced slowly backwards out of the door into the garden, which was full of moonlight and stillness. The vamped dress of silver paper and paste, which had been too glaring in the footlights, looked more and more magical and silvery as it danced away under a brilliant moon. The audience was closing in with a cataract of applause, when Brown felt his arm abruptly touched, and he was asked in a whisper to come into the colonel's study.

He followed his summoner with increasing doubt, which was not dispelled by a solemn comicality in the scene of the study. There sat Colonel Adams, still unaffectedly dressed as a pantaloon, with the knobbed whalebone nodding above his brow, but with his poor old eyes sad enough to have sobered a Saturnalia. Sir Leopold Fischer was leaning against the mantelpiece and heaving with all the importance of panic.

"This is a very painful matter, Father Brown," said Adams. "The truth is, those diamonds we all saw this afternoon seem to have vanished from my friend's tail-coat pocket. And as you——"

"As I," supplemented Father Brown, with a broad grin, "was sitting just behind him——"

"Nothing of the sort shall be suggested," said Colonel Adams, with a firm look at Fischer, which rather implied that some such thing *had* been suggested. "I only ask you to give me the assistance that any gentleman might give."

"Which is turning out his pockets," said Father Brown, and proceeded to do so, displaying seven and sixpence, a return ticket, a small silver crucifix, a small breviary, and a stick of chocolate.

The colonel looked at him long and then said: "Do you know, I should like to see the inside of your head more than the inside of your pockets. My daughter is one of your people, I know; well, she has lately——" and he stopped.

"She has lately," cried out old Fischer, "opened her father's house to a cut-throat Socialist, who says openly he would steal anything from a richer man. This is the end of it. Here is the richer man — and none the richer."

"If you want the inside of my head, you can have it," said Father Brown rather wearily. "What it's worth you can say afterwards. But the first thing I find in that disused pocket is this; that men who mean to steal diamonds don't talk Socialism. They are more likely," he added demurely, "to denounce it."

Both the others shifted sharply, and the priest went on:

"You see, we know these people, more or less. That Socialist would no more steal a diamond than a Pyramid. We ought to look at once to the one man we don't know. The fellow acting the policeman — Florian. Where is he exactly at this minute, I wonder?"

The pantaloon sprang erect and strode out of the room. An interlude ensued, during which the millionaire stared at the priest, and the priest at his breviary; then the pantaloon returned and said, with *staccato* gravity: "The policeman is still lying on the stage. The curtain has gone up and down six times; he is still lying there."

Father Brown dropped his book and stood staring with a look of blank mental ruin. Very slowly a light began to creep back in his grey eyes, and then he made the scarcely obvious answer.

"Please forgive me, colonel, but when did your wife die?"

"My wife!" replied the staring soldier, "she died this year two months. Her brother James arrived just a week too late to see her."

The little priest bounded like a rabbit shot. "Come on!" he cried in quite unusual excitement. "Come on! We've got to go and look at that policeman!"

They rushed on to the now curtained stage, breaking rudely past the columbine and clown (who seemed whispering quite contentedly), and Father Brown bent over the prostrate comic policeman.

"Chloroform," he said as he rose; "I only guessed it just now."

There was a startled stillness, and then the colonel said slowly: "Please say seriously what all this means."

Father Brown suddenly shouted with laughter, then stopped, and only struggled with it for instants during the rest of his speech. "Gentlemen," he gasped, "there's not much time to talk. I must run after the criminal. But this great French actor who played the policeman — this clever corpse the harlequin waltzed with and dandled and threw about — he was——" His voice again failed him, and he turned his back to run.

"He was?" called Fischer inquiringly.

"A real policeman," said Father Brown, and ran away, into the dark.

There were hollows and bowers at the extreme end of that leafy garden, in which the laurels and other immortal shrubs showed against sapphire sky and silver moon, even in that midwinter, warm colours as of the south. The green gaiety of the waving laurels, the rich purple indigo of the night, the moon like a monstrous crystal, make an almost irresponsibly romantic picture; and among the top branches of the garden trees a strange figure is climbing, who looks not so much romantic as impossible. He sparkles from head to heel, as if clad in ten million moons; the real moon catches him at every moment and sets a new inch of him on fire. But he swings, flashing and successful, from the short tree in this garden to the tall, rambling tree in the other, and only stops there because a shade has slid under the smaller tree and has unmistakably called up to him.

"Well, Flambeau," says the voice, "you really look like a Flying Star; but that always means a Falling Star at last."

The silver, sparkling figure above seems to lean forward in the laurels and, confident of escape, listens to the little figure below.

"You never did anything better, Flambeau. It was clever to come from Canada (with a Paris ticket, I suppose) just a week after Mrs Adams died, when no one was in a mood to ask questions. It was cleverer to have marked down the Flying Stars and the very day of Fischer's coming. But there's no cleverness, but mere genius, in what followed. Stealing the stones, I suppose, was nothing to you. You could have done it by sleight of hand in a hundred other ways besides that pretence of putting a paper donkey's tail to Fischer's coat. But in the rest you eclipsed yourself."

The silvery figure among the green leaves seems to linger as if hypnotised, though his escape is easy behind him; he is staring at the man below.

"Oh, yes," says the man below, "I know all about it. I know you not only forced the pantomime, but put it to a double use. You were going to steal the stones quietly; news came by an accomplice that you were already suspected, and a capable police-officer was coming to rout you up that very night. A common thief would have been thankful for the warning and fled; but you are a poet. You already had the clever notion of hiding the jewels in a blaze of false stage jewellery. Now, you saw that if the dress were a harlequin's the appearance of a policeman would be quite in keeping. The worthy officer started from Putney police station to find you, and walked into the queerest trap ever set in this world. When the front door opened he walked straight on to the stage of a Christmas pantomime, where he could be kicked, clubbed, stunned and drugged by the dancing harlequin, amid roars of laughter from all the most respectable people in Putney. Oh, you will never do anything better. And now, by the way, you might give me back those diamonds."

The green branch on which the glittering figure swung, rustled as if in astonishment; but the voice went on:

"I want you to give them back, Flambeau, and I want you to give up this life. There is still youth and honour and humour in you; don't fancy they will last in that trade. Men may keep a sort of level of good, but no man has ever been able to keep on one level of evil. That road goes down and down. The kind man drinks and turns cruel; the frank man kills and lies about it. Many a man I've known started like you to be an honest outlaw, a merry robber of the rich, and ended stamped with slime. Maurice Blum started out as an anarchist of principle, a father of the poor; he ended a greasy spy and tale-bearer that both sides used and despised. Harry Burke started his free money movement sincerely enough; now he's sponging on a half-starved sister for endless brandies and sodas. Lord Amber went into wild society in a sort of chivalry; now he's paying blackmail to the lowest

vultures in London. Captain Barillon was the great
gentleman-apache before your time; he died in a madhouse,
screaming with fear of the 'narks' and receivers that had
betrayed him and hunted him down. I know the woods look
very free behind you, Flambeau; I know that in a flash you
could melt into them like a monkey. But some day you will
be an old grey monkey, Flambeau. You will sit up in your
tree forest cold at heart and close to death, and the treetops
will be very bare."

Everything continued still, as if the small man below held
the other in the tree in some long invisible leash; and he went
on:

"Your downward steps have begun. You used to boast of
doing nothing mean, but you are doing something mean
tonight. You are leaving suspicion on an honest boy with a
good deal against him already; you are separating him from
the woman he loves and who loves him. But you will do
meaner things than that before you die."

Three flashing diamonds fell from the tree to the turf. The
small man stooped to pick them up, and when he looked up
again the green cage of the tree was emptied of its silver
bird.

The restoration of the gems (accidentally picked up by
Father Brown, of all people) ended the evening in uproarious
triumph; and Sir Leopold, in his height of good humour, even
told the priest that though he himself had broader views, he
could respect those whose creed required them to be
cloistered and ignorant of this world.

Robert Louis Stevenson

MARKHEIM

"**Y**ES," said the dealer, "our windfalls are of various kinds. Some customers are ignorant, and then I touch a dividend on my superior knowledge. Some are dishonest," and here he held up the candle, so that the light fell strongly on his visitor, "and in that case," he continued, "I profit by my virtue."

Markheim had but just entered from the daylight streets, and his eyes had not yet grown familiar with the mingled shine and darkness in the shop. At these pointed words, and before the near presence of the flame, he blinked painfully and looked aside.

The dealer chuckled. "You come to see me on Christmas Day," he resumed, "when you know that I am alone in my house, put up my shutters, and make a point of refusing business. Well, you will have to pay for that; you will have to pay for my loss of time, when I should be balancing my books; you will have to pay, besides, for a kind of manner that I remark in you today very strongly. I am the essence of discretion, and ask no awkward questions; but when a customer cannot look me in the eye, he has to pay for it." The dealer once more chuckled; and then, changing to his usual business voice, though still with a note of irony, "You can give, as usual, a clear account of how you came into the possession of the object?" he continued. "Still your uncle's cabinet? A remarkable collector, sir!"

And the little pale, round-shouldered dealer stood almost

on tip-toe, looking over the top of his gold spectacles, and nodding his head with every mark of disbelief. Markheim returned his gaze with one of infinite pity, and a touch of horror.

"This time," said he, "you are in error. I have not come to sell, but to buy. I have no curios to dispose of; my uncle's cabinet is bare to the wainscot; even were it still intact, I have done well on the Stock Exchange, and should more likely add to it than otherwise, and my errand today is simplicity itself. I seek a Christmas present for a lady," he continued, waxing more fluent as he struck into the speech he had prepared; "and certainly I owe you every excuse for thus disturbing you upon so small a matter. But the thing was neglected yesterday; I must produce my little compliment at dinner; and, as you very well know, a rich marriage is not a thing to be neglected."

There followed a pause, during which the dealer seemed to weigh this statement incredulously. The ticking of many clocks among the curious lumber of the shop, and the faint rushing of the cabs in a near thoroughfare, filled up the interval of silence.

"Well, sir," said the dealer, "be it so. You are an old customer after all; and if, as you say, you have the chance of a good marriage, far be it from me to be an obstacle. Here is a nice thing for a lady now," he went on, "this hand-glass — fifteenth century, warranted; comes from a good collection, too; but I reserve the name, in the interests of my customer, who was just like yourself, my dear sir, the nephew and sole heir of a remarkable collector."

The dealer, while he thus ran on in his dry and biting voice, had stooped to take the object from its place; and, as he had done so, a shock had passed through Markheim, a start both of hand and foot, a sudden leap of many tumultuous passions to the face. It passed as swiftly as it came, and left no trace beyond a certain trembling of the hand that now received the glass.

"A glass," he said hoarsely, and then paused, and repeated it more clearly. "A glass? For Christmas? Surely not?"

"And why not?" cried the dealer. "Why not a glass?"

Markheim was looking upon him with an indefinable expression. "You ask me why not?" he said. "Why, look here — look in it — look at yourself! Do you like to see it? No! nor I — nor any man."

The little man had jumped back when Markheim had so suddenly confronted him with the mirror; but now, perceiving there was nothing worse on hand, he chuckled. "Your future lady, sir, must be pretty hard favoured," said he.

"I ask you," said Markheim, "for a Christmas present, and you give me this — this damned reminder of years, and sins and follies — this hand-conscience! Did you mean it? Had you a thought in your mind? Tell me. It will be better for you if you do. Come, tell me about yourself. I hazard a guess now, that you are in secret a very charitable man?"

The dealer looked closely at his companion. It was very odd. Markheim did not appear to be laughing; there was something in his face like an eager sparkle of hope, but nothing of mirth.

"What are you driving at?" the dealer asked.

"Not charitable?" returned the other gloomily. "Not charitable; not pious; not scrupulous; unloving, unbeloved; a hand to get money, a safe to keep it. Is that all? Dear God, man, is that all?"

"I will tell you what it is," began the dealer, with some sharpness, and then broke off again into a chuckle. "But I see this is a love-match of yours, and you have been drinking the lady's health."

"Ah!" cried Markheim, with a strange curiosity. "Ah, have you been in love? Tell me about that."

"I," cried the dealer. "I in love! I never had the time, nor have I the time today for all this nonsense. Will you take the glass?"

"Where is the hurry?" returned Markheim. "It is very pleasant to stand here talking; and life is so short and insecure that I would not hurry away from any pleasure — no, not even from so mild a one as this. We should rather cling, cling to what little we can get, like a man at a cliff's edge. Every second is a cliff, if you think upon it — a cliff a mile high — high enough, if we fall, to dash us out of every feature of humanity. Hence it is best to talk pleasantly. Let us talk of each other: why should we wear this mask? Let us be confidential. Who knows, we might become friends?"

"I have just one word to say to you," said the dealer. "Either make your purchase, or walk out of my shop!"

"True, true," said Markheim. "Enough fooling. To business. Show me something else."

The dealer stooped once more, this time to replace the glass upon the shelf, his thin blond hair falling over his eyes as he did so. Markheim moved a little nearer, with one hand in the pocket of his greatcoat; he drew himself up and filled his lungs; at the same time many different emotions were depicted together on his face — terror, horror, and resolve, fascination and a physical repulsion; and through a haggard lift of his upper lip, his teeth looked out.

"This, perhaps, may suit," observed the dealer: and then, as he began to re-arise, Markheim bounded from behind upon his victim. The long skewerlike dagger flashed and fell. The dealer struggled like a hen, striking his temple on the shelf, and then tumbled on the floor in a heap.

Time had some score of small voices in that shop, some stately and slow as was becoming to their great age; others garrulous and hurried. All these told out the seconds in an intricate chorus of tickings. Then the passage of a lad's feet, heavily running on the pavement, broke in upon these smaller voices and startled Markheim into the consciousness of his surroundings. He looked about him awfully. The candle stood on the counter, its flame solemnly wagging in a draught; and by that inconsiderable movement, the whole

room was filled with noiseless bustle and kept heaving like a
sea; the tall shadows nodding, the gross blots of darkness
swelling and dwindling as with respiration, the faces of the
portraits and the china gods changing and wavering like
images in water. The inner door stood ajar, and peered into
that leaguer of shadows with a long slit of daylight like a
pointing finger.

From these fear-stricken rovings Markheim's eye
returned to the body of his victim, where it lay both humped
and sprawling, incredibly small and strangely meaner than in
life. In these poor, miserly clothes, in that ungainly attitude,
the dealer lay like so much sawdust. Markheim had feared to
see it, and lo! it was nothing. And yet, as he gazed, this
bundle of old clothes and pool of blood began to find
eloquent voices. There it must lie; there was none to work
the cunning hinges or direct the miracle of locomotion —
there it must lie till it was found. Found! ay, and then? Then
would his dead flesh lift up a cry that would ring over
England, and fill the world with the echoes of pursuit. Ay,
dead or not, this was still the enemy. "Time was that when
the brains were out," he thought; and the first word struck
into his mind. Time, now that the deed was accomplished —
time, which had closed for the victim, had become instant
and momentous for the slayer.

The thought was yet in his mind, when, first one and then
another, with every variety of pace and voice — one deep as
the bell from a cathedral turret, another ringing on its treble
notes the prelude of a waltz — the clocks began to strike the
hour of three in the afternoon.

The sudden outbreak of so many tongues in that dumb
chamber staggered him. He began to bestir himself, going to
and fro with the candle, beleaguered by moving shadows,
and startled to the soul by chance reflections. In many rich
mirrors, some of home design, some from Venice or
Amsterdam, he saw his own face repeated and repeated, as it
were an army of spies; his own eyes met and detected him;

and the sound of his own steps, lightly as they fell, vexed the surrounding quiet. And still, as he continued to fill his pockets, his mind accused him with a sickening iteration of the thousand faults of his design. He should have chosen a more quiet hour; he should have prepared an alibi; he should not have used a knife; he should have been more cautious and only bound and gagged the dealer, and not killed him; he should have been more bold and killed the servant also; he should have done all things otherwise; poignant regrets, weary, incessant toiling of the mind to change what was unchangeable, to plan what was now useless, to be the architect of the irrevocable past. Meanwhile, and behind all this activity, brute terrors, like the scurrying of rats in a deserted attic, filled the more remote chambers of his brain with riot; the hand of the constable would fall heavy on his shoulder, and his nerves would jerk like a hooked fish; or he beheld, in galloping defile, the dock, the prison, the gallows, and the black coffin.

Terror of the people in the street sat down before his mind like a besieging army. It was impossible, he thought, but that some rumour of the struggle must have reached their ears and set on edge their curiosity; and now, in all the neighbouring houses, he divined them sitting motionless and with uplifted ear — solitary people, condemned to spend Christmas dwelling alone on memories of the past, and now startlingly recalled from that tender exercise; happy family parties, struck into silence round the table, the mother still with raised finger: every degree and age and humour, but all, by their own hearths, prying and hearkening and weaving the rope that was to hang him. Sometimes it seemed to him he could not move too softly; the clink of the tall Bohemian goblets rang out loudly like a bell; and alarmed by the bigness of the ticking, he was tempted to stop the clocks. And then, again, with a swift transition of his terrors, the very silence of the place appeared a source of peril, and a thing to strike and freeze the passer-by; and he would step more boldly, and bustle aloud among the contents of the shop and imitate, with elaborate bravado, the movements of a busy man at ease in his own house.

But he was now so pulled about by different alarms that, while one portion of his mind was still alert and cunning, another trembled on the brink of lunacy. One hallucination in particular took a strong hold on his credulity. The neighbour hearkening with white face beside his window, the passer-by arrested by a horrible surmise on the pavement — these could at worst suspect, they could not know; through the brick walls and shuttered windows only sounds could penetrate. But here, within the house, was he alone? He knew he was; he had watched the servant set forth sweethearting, in her poor best, "out for the day" written in every ribbon and smile. Yes, he was alone, of course; and yet, in the bulk of empty house above him, he could surely hear a stir of delicate footing — he was surely conscious, inexplicably conscious of some presence. Ay, surely; to every room and corner of the house his imagination followed it; and now it was a faceless thing, and yet had eyes to see with; and again it was a shadow of himself; and yet again behold the image of the dead dealer, reinspired with cunning and hatred.

At times, with a strong effort, he would glance at the open door which still seemed to repel his eyes. The house was tall, the skylight small and dirty, the day blind with fog; and the light that filtered down to the ground storey was exceedingly faint, and showed dimly on the threshold of the shop. And yet, in that strip of doubtful brightness, did there not hang wavering a shadow?

Suddenly, from the street outside, a very jovial gentleman began to beat with a staff on the shop door, accompanying his blows with shouts and railleries in which the dealer was continually called upon by name. Markheim, smitten into ice, glanced at the dead man. But no! he lay quite still; he was fled away far beyond earshot of these blows and shoutings;

he was sunk beneath seas of silence; and his name, which would once have caught his notice above the howling of a storm, had become an empty sound. And presently the jovial gentleman desisted from his knocking and departed.

Here was a broad hint to hurry what remained to be done, to get forth from this accusing neighbourhood, to plunge into a bath of London multitudes, and to reach, on the other side of day, that haven of safety and apparent innocence — his bed. One visitor had come: at any moment another might follow and be more obstinate. To have done the deed, and yet not to reap the profit, would be too abhorrent a failure. The money, that was now Markheim's concern; and as a means to that, the keys.

He glanced over his shoulder at the open door, where the shadow was still lingering and shivering; and with no conscious repugnance of the mind, yet with a tremor of the belly, he drew near the body of his victim. The human character had quite departed. Like a suit half-stuffed with bran, the limbs lay scattered, the trunk doubled, on the floor; and yet the thing repelled him. Although so dingy and inconsiderable to the eye, he feared it might have more significance to the touch. He took the body by the shoulders and turned it on its back. It was strangely light and supple, and the limbs, as if they had been broken, fell into the oddest postures. The face was robbed of all expression; but it was as pale as wax, and shockingly smeared with blood about one temple. That was, for Markheim, the one displeasing circumstance. It carried him back, upon the instant, to a certain fair-day in a fishers' village: a grey day, a piping wind, a crowd upon the street, the blare of brasses, the booming of drums, the nasal voice of a ballad singer; and a boy going to and fro, buried over head in the crowd and divided between interest and fear, until, coming out on the chief place of concourse, he beheld a booth and a great screen with pictures, dismally designed, garishly coloured: Brownrigg with her apprentice; the Mannings with their

murdered guest; Weare in the death-grip of Thurtell; and a
score besides of famous crimes. The thing was as clear as an
illusion; he was once again that little boy; he was looking
once again, and with the same sense of physical revolt, at
these vile pictures; he was still stunned by the thumping of
the drums. A bar of that day's music returned upon his
memory; and at that, for the first time, a qualm came over
him, a breath of nausea, a sudden weakness of the joints,
which he must instantly resist and conquer.

He judged it more prudent to confront than to flee from
these considerations; looking the more hardily in the dead
face, bending his mind to realise the nature and greatness of
his crime. So little a while ago that face had moved with
every change of sentiment, that pale mouth had spoken, that
body had been all on fire with governable energies; and now,
and by his act, that piece of life had been arrested, as the
horologist, with interjected finger, arrests the beating of the
clock. So he reasoned in vain; he could rise to no more
remorseful consciousness; the same heart which had
shuddered before the painted effigies of crime, looked on its
reality unmoved. At best, he felt a gleam of pity for one who
had been endowed in vain with all those faculties that can
make the world a garden of enchantment, one who had
never lived and who was now dead. But of penitence, no, not
a tremor.

With that, shaking himself clear of these considerations,
he found the keys and advanced towards the open door of the
shop. Outside, it had begun to rain smartly; and the sound of
the shower upon the roof had banished silence. Like some
dripping cavern, the chambers of the house were haunted by
an incessant echoing, which filled the ear and mingled with
the ticking of the clocks. And, as Markheim approached the
door, he seemed to hear, in answer to his own cautious tread,
the steps of another foot withdrawing up the stair. The
shadow still palpitated loosely on the threshold. He threw a

ton's weight of resolve upon his muscles, and drew back the door.

The faint, foggy daylight glimmered dimly on the bare floor and stairs; on the bright suit of armour posted, halbert in hand, upon the landing; and on the dark wood-carvings and framed pictures that hung against the yellow panels of the wainscot. So loud was the beating of the rain through all the house, that, in Markheim's ears, it began to be distinguished into many different sounds. Footsteps and sighs, the tread of regiments marching in the distance, the chink of money in the counting, and the creaking of doors held stealthily ajar, appeared to mingle with the patter of drops upon the cupola and the gushing of the water in the pipes. The sense that he was not alone grew upon him to the verge of madness. On every side he was haunted and begirt by presences. He heard them moving in the upper chambers; from the shop, he heard the dead man getting to his legs; and as he began with a great effort to mount the stairs, feet fled quietly before him and followed stealthily behind. If he were but deaf, he thought, how tranquilly he would possess his soul! And then again, and hearkening with ever fresh attention, he blessed himself for that unresting sense which held the outposts and stood a trusty sentinel upon his life. His head turned continually on his neck; his eyes, which seemed starting from their orbits, scouted on every side, and on every side were half-rewarded as with the tail of something nameless vanishing. The four-and-twenty steps to the first floor were four-and-twenty agonies.

On that first storey the doors stood ajar, three of them like three ambushes, shaking his nerves like the throats of cannon. He could never again, he felt, be sufficiently immured and fortified from men's observing eyes; he longed to be home, girt in by walls, buried among bedclothes, and invisible to all but God. And at that thought he wondered a little, recollecting tales of other murderers and the fear they were said to entertain of heavenly avengers. It was not so, at least, with him. He feared the laws of nature, lest in their callous and immutable procedure they should preserve some damning evidence of his crime. He feared tenfold more, with a slavish, superstitious terror, some scission in the continuity of man's experience, some wilful illegality of nature. He played a game of skill, depending on the rules, calculating consequence from cause; and what if nature, as the defeated tyrant overthrew the chessboard, should break the mould of their succession? The like had befallen Napoleon (so writers said) when the winter changed the time of its appearance. The like might befall Markheim; the solid walls might become transparent and reveal his doings like those of bees in a glass hive; the stout planks might yield under his foot like quicksands and detain him in their clutch; ay, and there were soberer accidents that might destroy him; if, for instance, the house should fall and imprison him beside the body of his victim; or the house next door should fly on fire, and the firemen invade him from all sides. These things he feared; and, in a sense, these things might be called the hands of God reached forth against sin. But about God Himself he was at ease; his act was doubtless exceptional, but so were his excuses, which God knew; it was there, and not among men, that he felt sure of justice.

When he had got safe into the drawing-room and shut the door behind him, he was aware of a respite from alarms. The room was quite dismantled, uncarpeted besides, and strewn with packing-cases and incongruous furniture; several great pier-glasses, in which he beheld himself at various angles, like an actor on a stage; many pictures, framed and unframed, standing, with their faces to the wall; a fine Sheraton sideboard, a cabinet of marquetry, and a great old bed, with tapestry hangings. The windows opened to the floor; but by great good fortune the lower part of the shutters had been closed, and this concealed him from the neighbours. Here, then, Markheim drew in a packing-case before the cabinet and began to search among the keys. It was a long business, for there were many, and it was irksome, besides; for, after all, there might be nothing in the cabinet, and time was on the wing. But the closeness of the occupation sobered him. With the tail of his eye he saw the door — even glanced at it from time to time directly, like a besieged commander pleased to verify the good estate of his defences. But in truth he was at peace. The rain falling in the street sounded natural and pleasant. Presently, on the other side, the notes of a piano were wakened to the music of a hymn, and the voices of many children took up the air and words. How stately, how comfortable was the melody! How fresh the youthful voices! Markheim gave ear to it smilingly, as he sorted out the keys; and his mind was thronged with answerable ideas and images; church-going children and the pealing of the high organ; children afield, bathers by the brookside, ramblers on the brambly common, kite-fliers in the windy and cloud-navigated sky; and then, at another cadence of the hymn, back again to church, and the somnolence of summer Sundays, and the high genteel voice of the parson (which he smiled a little to recall), and the painted Jacobean tombs, and the dim lettering of the Ten Commandments in the chancel.

And as he sat thus, at once busy and absent, he was startled to his feet. A flash of ice, a flash of fire, a bursting gush of blood, went over him, and then he stood transfixed and thrilling. A step mounted the stair slowly and steadily, and presently a hand was laid upon the knob, the lock clicked, and the door opened.

Fear held Markheim in a vice. What to expect he knew not, whether the dead man walking, or the official ministers of human justice, or some chance witness blindly stumbling in to consign him to the gallows. But when a face was thrust into the aperture, glanced round the room, looked at him, nodded and smiled as if in friendly recognition, and then withdrew again, and the door closed behind it, his fear broke loose from his control in a hoarse cry. At the sound of this the visitant returned.

"Did you call me?" he asked pleasantly, and with that he entered the room and closed the door behind him.

Markheim stood and gazed at him with all his eyes. Perhaps there was a film upon his sight, but the outlines of the newcomer seemed to change and waver like those of the idols in the wavering candlelight of the shop; and at times he thought he knew him; and at times he thought he bore a likeness to himself; and always, like a lump of living terror, there lay in his bosom the conviction that this thing was not of the earth and not of God.

And yet the creature had a strange air of the common-place, as he stood looking on Markheim with a smile; and when he added: "You are looking for the money, I believe?" it was in the tones of everyday politeness.

Markheim made no answer.

"I should warn you," resumed the other, "that the maid has left her sweetheart earlier than usual and will soon be here. If Mr Markheim be found in this house, I need not describe to him the consequences."

"You know me?" cried the murderer.

The visitor smiled. "You have long been a favourite of mine," he said; "and I have long observed and often sought to help you."

"What are you?" cried Markheim: "the Devil?"

"What I may be," returned the other, "cannot affect the service I propose to render you."

"It can," cried Markheim; "it does! Be helped by you? No, never; not by you! You do not know me yet; thank God, you do not know me!"

"I know you," replied the visitant, with a sort of kind severity or rather firmness. "I know you to the soul."

"Know me!" cried Markheim. "Who can do so? My life is but a travesty and slander on myself. I have lived to belie my nature. All men do; all men are better than this disguise that grows about and stifles them. You see each dragged away by life, like one whom bravos have seized and muffled in a cloak. If they had their own control — if you could see their faces, they would be altogether different, they would shine out for heroes and saints! I am worse than most; myself is more overlaid; my excuse is known to me and God. But, had I the time, I could disclose myself."

"To me?" inquired the visitant.

"To you before all," returned the murderer. "I supposed you were intelligent. I thought — since you exist — you would prove a reader of the heart. And yet you would propose to judge me by my acts! Think of it; my acts! I was born and I have lived in a land of giants; giants have dragged me by the wrists since I was born out of my mother — the giants of circumstance. And you would judge me by my acts! But can you not look within? Can you not understand that evil is hateful to me? Can you not see within me the clear writing of conscience, never blurred by any wilful sophistry, although too often disregarded? Can you not read me for a thing that surely must be common as humanity — the unwilling sinner?"

"All this is very feelingly expressed," was the reply, "but it regards me not. These points of consistency are beyond my province, and I care not in the least by what compulsion you may have been dragged away, so as you are but carried in the right direction. But time flies; the servant delays, looking in the faces of the crowd and at the pictures on the hoardings, but still she keeps moving nearer; and remember, it is as if the gallows itself was striding towards you through the Christmas streets! Shall I help you; I, who know all? Shall I tell you where to find the money?"

"For what price?" asked Markheim.

"I offer you the service for a Christmas gift," returned the other.

Markheim could not refrain from smiling with a kind of bitter triumph. "No," said he, "I will take nothing at your hands; if I were dying of thirst, and it was your hand that put the pitcher to my lips, I should find the courage to refuse. It may be credulous, but I will do nothing to commit myself to evil."

"I have no objection to a death-bed repentance," observed the visitant.

"Because you disbelieve their efficacy!" Markheim cried.

"I do not say so," returned the other; "but I look on these things from a different side, and when the life is done my interest falls. The man has lived to serve me, to spread black looks under colour of religion, or to sow tares in the wheatfield, as you do, in a course of weak compliance with desire. Now that he draws so near to his deliverance, he can add but one act of service — to repent, to die smiling, and thus to build up in confidence and hope the more timorous of my surviving followers. I am not so hard a master. Try me. Accept my help. Please yourself in life as you have done hitherto; please yourself more amply, spread your elbows at the board; and when the night begins to fall and the curtains to be drawn, I tell you, for your greater comfort, that you will find it even easy to compound your quarrel with your conscience, and to make a truckling peace with God. I came but now from such a death-bed, and the room was full of sincere mourners, listening to the man's last words: and when I looked into that face, which had been set as a flint against mercy, I found it smiling with hope."

"And do you, then, suppose me such a creature?" asked Markheim. "Do you think I have no more generous aspirations than to sin, and sin, and sin, and, at the last, sneak into heaven? My heart rises at the thought. Is this, then, your experience of mankind? or is it because you find me with red hands that you presume such baseness? and is this crime of murder indeed so impious as to dry up the very springs of good?"

"Murder is to me no special category," replied the other. "All sins are murder, even as all life is war. I behold your race, like starving mariners on a raft, plucking crusts out of the hands of famine and feeding on each other's lives. I follow sins beyond the moment of their acting; I find in all that the last consequence is death; and to my eyes, the pretty maid who thwarts her mother with such taking graces on a question of a ball, drips no less visibly with human gore than such a murderer as yourself. Do I say that I follow sins? I follow virtues also; they differ not by the thickness of a nail, they are both scythes for the reaping angel of Death. Evil, for which I live, consists not in action but in character. The bad man is dear to me; not the bad act, whose fruits, if we could follow them far enough down the hurtling cataract of the ages, might yet be found more blessed than those of the rarest virtues. And it is not because you have killed a dealer, but because you are Markheim, that I offer to forward your escape."

"I will lay my heart open to you," answered Markheim. "This crime on which you find me is my last. On my way to it I have learned many lessons; itself is a lesson, a momentous lesson. Hitherto I have been driven with revolt to what I would not; I was a bond-slave to poverty, driven and scourged. There are robust virtues that can stand in these temptations; mine was no so: I had a thirst of pleasure. But today, and out of this deed, I pluck both warning and riches — both the power and a fresh resolve to be myself. I become in all things a free actor in the world; I begin to see myself all changed, these hands the agents of good, this heart at peace. Something comes over me out of the past; something of what I have dreamed on Sabbath evenings to the sound of the church organ, of what I forecast when I shed tears over noble books, or talked, an innocent child, with my mother. There lies my life; I have wandered a few years, but now I see once more my city of destination."

"You are to use this money on the Stock Exchange, I think?" remarked the visitor; "and there, if I mistake not, you have already lost some thousands?"

"Ah," said Markheim, "but this time I have a sure thing."

"This time, again, you will lose," replied the visitor quietly.

"Ah, but I keep back the half!" cried Markheim.

"That also you will lose," said the other.

The sweat started upon Markheim's brow. "Well, then, what matter?" he exclaimed. "Say it be lost, say I am plunged again in poverty, shall one part of me, and that the worse, continue until the end to override the better? Evil and good run strong in me, haling me both ways. I do not love the one thing, I love all. I can conceive great deeds, renunciations, martyrdoms; and though I be fallen to such a crime as murder, pity is no stranger to my thoughts. I pity the poor; who knows their trials better than myself? I pity and help them; I prize love, I love honest laughter; there is no good thing nor true thing on earth but I love it from my heart. And are my vices only to direct my life, and my virtues to lie without effect, like some passive lumber of the mind? Not so; good, also, is a spring of acts."

But the visitant raised his finger. "For six-and-thirty years that you have been in this world," said he, "through many changes of fortune and varieties of humour, I have watched you steadily fall. Fifteen years ago you would have started at a theft. Three years back you would have blenched at the name of murder. Is there any crime, is there any cruelty or meanness, from which you still recoil? — five years from now I shall detect you in the fact! Downward, downward, lies your way; nor can anything but death avail to stop you."

"It is true," Markheim said huskily, "I have in some degree complied with evil. But it is so with all; the very saints, in the mere exercise of living, grow less dainty, and take on the tone of their surroundings."

"I will propound to you one simple question," said the other; "and as you answer, I shall read to you your moral horoscope. You have grown in many things more lax;

possibly you do right to be so; and at any account, it is the same with all men. But granting that, are you in any one particular, however trifling, more difficult to please with your own conduct, or do you go in all things with a looser rein?"

"In any one?" repeated Markheim, with an anguish of consideration. "No," he added, with despair, "in none! I have gone down in all."

"Then," said the visitor, "content yourself with what you are, for you will never change; and the words of your part on this stage are irrevocably written down."

Markheim stood for a long while silent, and indeed it was the visitor who first broke the silence. "That being so," he said, "shall I show you the money?"

"And grace?" cried Markheim.

"Have you not tried it?" returned the other. "Two or three years ago, did I not see you on the platform of revival meetings, and was not your voice the loudest in the hymn?"

"It is true," said Markheim; "and I see clearly what remains for me by way of duty. I thank you for these lessons from my soul; my eyes are opened, and I behold myself at last for what I am."

At this moment the sharp note of the doorbell rang through the house; and the visitant, as though this were some concerted signal for which he had been waiting, changed at once in his demeanour.

"The maid!" he cried. "She has returned, as I forewarned you, and there is now before you one more difficult passage. Her master, you must say, is ill; you must let her in, with an assured but rather serious countenance — no smiles, no over-acting, and I promise you success! Once the girl within, and the door closed, the same dexterity that has already rid you of the dealer will relieve you of this last danger in your path. Thenceforward you have the whole evening — the whole night, if needful — to ransack the treasures of the house and to make good your safety. This is help that comes to you with the mask of danger. Up!" he cried; "up, friend; your life hangs trembling in the scales: up, and act!"

Markheim steadily regarded his counsellor. "If I be condemned to evil acts," he said, "there is still one door of freedom open — I can cease action. If my life be an ill thing, I can lay it down. Though I be, as you say truly, at the beck of every small temptation, I can yet, by one decisive gesture, place myself beyond the reach of all. My love of good is damned to barrenness; it may, and let it be! But I have still my hatred of evil; and from that, to your galling disappointment, you shall see that I can draw both energy and courage."

The features of the visitor began to undergo a wonderful and lovely change: they brightened and softened with a tender triumph, and, even as they brightened, faded and dislimned. But Markheim did not pause to watch or understand the transformation. He opened the door and went downstairs very slowly, thinking to himself. His past went soberly before him; he beheld it as it was, ugly and strenuous like a dream, random as chance-medley — a scene of defeat. Life, as he thus reviewed it, tempted him no longer; but on the farther side he perceived a quiet haven for his bark. He paused in the passage and looked into the shop, where the candle still burned by the dead body. It was strangely silent. Thoughts of the dealer swarmed into his mind as he stood gazing. And then the bell once more broke out into impatient clamour.

He confronted the maid upon the threshold with something like a smile.

"You had better go for the police," said he: "I have killed your master."

Robert Louis Stevenson

CHRISTMAS AT SEA

THE sheets were frozen hard, and they cut the naked
   hand;
The decks were like a slide, where a seaman scare could
   stand;
The wind was a nor'wester, blowing squally off the sea;
And cliffs and spouting breakers were the only things a-lee.

They heard the surf a-roaring before the break of day;
But 'twas only with the peep of light we saw how ill we lay.
We tumbled every hand on deck instanter, with a shout,
And we gave her the maintops'l, and stood by to go about.

All day we tacked and tacked between the South Head and
   the North;
All day we hauled the frozen sheets, and got no further forth;
All day as cold as charity, in bitter pain and dread,
For very life and nature we tacked from head to head.

We gave the South a wider berth, for there the tide race
   roared;
But every tack we made we brought the North Head close
   aboard:
So's we saw the cliffs and houses, and the breakers running
   high,
And the coastguard in his garden, with his glass against his
   eye.

The frost was on the village roofs as white as ocean foam;
The good red fires were burning bright in ev'ry longshore
    home;
The windows sparkled clear, and the chimneys volleyed out;
And I vow we sniffed the victuals as the vessel went about.

The bells upon the church were rung with a mighty jovial
    cheer;
For it's just that I should tell you how (of all days in the
    year)
This day of our adversity was blessed Christmas morn,
And the house above the coastguard's was the house where I
    was born.

O well I saw the pleasant room, the pleasant faces there,
My mother's silver spectacles, my father's silver hair;
And well I saw the firelight, like a flight of homely elves,
Go dancing round the china-plates that stand upon the
    shelves.

And well I knew the talk they had, the talk that was of me,
Of the shadow on the household and the son that went to sea;
And O the wicked fool I seemed, in every kind of way,
To be here and hauling frozen ropes on blessed Christmas
    Day.

They lit the high sea-light, and the dark began to fall.
"All hands to loose topgallant sails," I heard the captain
    call.
"By the Lord, she'll never stand it," our first mate, Jackson,
    cried.
. . . "It's the one way or the other, Mr Jackson," he replied.

She staggered to her bearings, but the sails were new and
    good,
And the ship smelt up to windward just as though she
    understood.

As the winter's day was ending, in the entry of the night,
We cleared the weary headland, and passed below the light.

And they heaved a mighty breath, every soul on board but
    me,
As they saw her nose again pointing handsome out to sea
But all that I could think of, in the darkness and the cold,
Was just that I was leaving home and my folks were growing
    old.

Rudyard Kipling

CHRISTMAS IN INDIA

D IM dawn behind the tamarisks—the sky is saffron-
        yellow—
  As the women in the village grind the corn,
And the parrots seek the river-side, each calling to his
      fellow
  That the Day, the staring Eastern Day, is born.
      O the white dust on the highway! O the stenches in
        the byway!
      O the clammy fog that hovers over earth!
      And at Home they're making merry 'neath the white
        and scarlet berry—
      What part have India's exiles in their mirth?

Full day behind the tamarisks—the sky is blue and
      staring—
  As the cattle crawl afield beneath the yoke,
And they bear One o'er the field-path, who is past all
      hope or caring,
  To the ghat below the curling wreaths of smoke.
      Call on Rama, going slowly, as ye bear a brother
        lowly—
      Call on Rama—he may hear, perhaps, your voice!
      With our hymn-books and our psalters we appeal to
        other altars,
      And today we bid "good Christian men rejoice!"

High noon behind the tamarisks—the sun is hot above us—
    As at Home the Christmas Day is breaking wan.
They will drink our healths at dinner—those who tell us how
        they love us,
    And forget us till another year be gone!
      O the toil that knows no breaking! O the *Heimweh*,
        ceaseless, aching!
      O the black dividing Sea and alien Plain!
     Youth was cheap—wherefore we sold it. Gold was
       good—we hoped to hold it.
     And today we know the fulness of our gain!

Grey dusk behind the tamarisks—the parrots fly together—
    As the Sun is sinking slowly over Home;
And his last ray seems to mock us shackled in a lifelong tether
    That drags us back howe'er so far we roam.
      Hard her service, poor her payment—she in ancient,
        tattered raiment—
      India, she the grim Stepmother of our kind.
     If a year of life be lent her, if her temple's shrine we
       enter,
      The door is shut—we may not look behind.

Black night behind the tamarisks—the owls begin their
        chorus—
    As the conches from the temple scream and bray.
With the fruitless years behind us and the hopeless years
        before us,
    Let us honour, O my brothers, Christmas Day!
      Call a truce, then, to our labours—let us feast with
        friends and neighbours,
      And be merry as the custom of our caste;
     For, if "faint and forced the laughter", and if sadness
       follow after,
      We are richer by one mocking Christmas past.

Arthur Conan Doyle

AN EXCITING
CHRISTMAS EVE
OR, MY LECTURE ON DYNAMITE

I

IT has often seemed to me to be a very strange and curious thing that danger and trouble should follow those who are most anxious to lead a quiet and uneventful life. I myself have been such a one, and I find on looking back that it was in those very periods of my existence which might have been most confidently reckoned on as peaceful that some unexpected adventure has befallen me, like the thunderbolt from an unclouded sky which shook the nerves of old Horace. Possibly my experience differs from that of other men, and I may have been especially unfortunate. If so, there is the more reason why I should mourn over my exceptional lot, and record it for the benefit of those more happily circumstanced.

Just compare my life with that of Leopold Walderich, and you will see what I complain of. We both come from Mulhausen, in Baden, and that is why I single him out as an example, though many others would do as well. He was a man who professed to be fond of adventure. Now listen to what occurred. We went to Heidelberg University together. I was quiet, studious, and unassuming; he was impetuous, reckless, and idle. For three years he revelled in every sort of riot, while I frequented the laboratories, and rarely deserted my books save for a hurried walk into the country when a pain in my head and ringing in my ears warned me that I was trifling with my constitution.

Yet during that period his life was comparatively uneventful, while my whole existence was a series of hair-breadth perils and escapes. I damaged my eyesight and nearly choked myself by the evolution of a poisonous gas. I swallowed a trichina in my ham, and was prostrated for weeks. I was hurled out of a second-floor window by an English lunatic because I ventured to quote the solemn and serious passage in Schoppheim's "Weltgeschichte" which proves Waterloo to have been a purely Prussian victory, and throws grave doubts on the presence of any British force nearer than Brussels! Twice I was nearly drowned, and once I should have been precipitated from the parapet of the schloss but for the assistance of this same Englishman. These are a few of the incidents which occurred to me while endeavouring to read in seclusion for my degree.

Even in smaller matters this luck of mine held good. I can well remember, for example, that on one occasion the wilder spirits of the Badischer Corps ventured upon an unusually hare-brained escapade. There was a farmer about a couple of miles from the town whose name was Nicholas Bodeck. This man had made himself obnoxious to the students, and they determined to play a prank upon him in return. An enormous number of little caps were accordingly made with the colours of the corps upon them, and the conspirators invaded his premises in the middle of the night and gummed them upon the heads of all the fowls.

They certainly had a very comical effect, as I had an opportunity of judging, for I happened to pass that way in the morning. I suppose that Walderich and his friends carried out their little joke for excitement, knowing the farmer to be a resolute man. *They* got no excitement from it, however; it was I who got that. Activity was never my strong point, but certainly I ran those two miles that morning with incredible speed — and so did the five men with pitchforks who ran behind me!

These things may seem trivial, but, as you say in England, a straw shows which way the wind blows, and these were only indications of what was to come.

I took my degree in medicine, and found myself Herr Doctor Otto von Spee. I then graduated in science, receiving much applause for my thesis, "On the Explosive Compounds of the Tri-methyl Series". I was quoted as an authority in works of science, and my professors prophesied that a great career lay before me. My studies, however, were suddenly put an end to by the outbreak of the great war with France.

Walderich volunteered into one of the crack regiments, fought in nearly every engagement, covered himself with glory, and came back unhurt to be decorated with the cross for valour. I was stationed in an ambulance which never even crossed the frontier, yet I succeeded in breaking my arm by tumbling over a stretcher, and in contracting erysipelas from one of the few wounds which came under my care. I got no medal or cross, and went back quietly to Berlin after it was all over, and there I settled as *privat docent* of chemistry and physics.

You will naturally ask what all this has to with my Christmas story. You shall see in time that it is necessary I should tell you this, in order that you may appreciate that crowning event in my long list of misfortunes. You must remember also that I am a German and therefore somewhat long-winded perhaps, as my nation has the reputation of being. I have often admired the dashing, rattling manner of English storytellers, but I fear if I were to attempt to imitate this it would be as if one of our own ponderous old Mulhausen storks were to adopt the pretty graceful airs of your Christmas robins. You shall hear in time all that I have to say about my Christmas Eve.

II

After I had settled in Berlin I endeavoured to combine the private practice of medicine with my labours as a *privat docent*, which corresponds to what you call a "coach" in England. For some years I pursued this plan, but I found that my practice, being largely among the lower classes, favoured my unfortunate propensity for getting into trouble, and I determined to abandon it.

I took a secluded house, therefore, in a quiet quarter of the city, and there I gave myself up to scientific research, pursuing principally the same train of investigation which had originally attracted me — namely, the chemistry of explosive compounds.

My expenses were small, and all the money which I could spare was laid out on scientific instruments and mechanical contrivances of different sorts. Soon I had a snug little laboratory which, if not as pretentious as that at Heidelberg, was quite as well fitted to supply my wants. It is true that the neighbours grumbled, and that Gretchen, my housekeeper, had to be quieted with a five-mark piece, after having been blown up three several times, and blown down once while engaged in fixing an electric wire upon the summit of an outhouse. These little matters, however, were easily settled, and I found my life rapidly assuming a peaceful complexion, of which I had long despaired.

I was happy — and what is more I was becoming famous. My "Remarks on Cacodyl" in the "Monthly Archives of Science" created no small sensation, and Herr Raubenthal of Bonn characterised them as "meisterlich", though dissenting from many of my deductions. I was enabled, however, in a later contribution to the same journal to recount certain experiments which were sufficient to convince that eminent *savant* that my view of the matter was the correct one.

After this victory I was universally recognised as an

authority in my own special branch, and as one of the foremost living workers at explosives. The Government appointed me to the torpedo commission at Kiel, and many other honours were bestowed upon me. One of the consequences of this sudden accession of celebrity was that I found myself in great request as a lecturer, both at scientific gatherings and at those meetings for the education of the people which have become so common in the metropolis. By these means my name got into the daily papers as one learned in such matters, and to this it is that I ascribe the events which I am about to narrate.

It was a raw windy Christmas Eve. The sleet pattered against the window panes, and the blast howled among the skeleton branches of the gaunt poplar trees in my garden. There were few people in the street, and those few had their coats buttoned up, and their chins upon their breasts, and hurried rapidly homewards, staggering along against the force of the storm. Even the big policeman outside had ceased to clank up and down, and was crouching in a doorway for protection.

Many a lonely man might have felt uncomfortable upon such a night, but I was too interested in my work to have time for any sympathy with the state of the weather. A submarine mine was engaging my attention, and in a leaden tank in front of me I had sunk a small pellet of my new explosive. The problem was how far its destructive capacities would be modified by the action of the water. The matter was too important to allow me to feel despondent. Besides, one of Gretchen's lovers was in the kitchen, and his gruff expressions of satisfaction, whether with her charms or my beer, or both, were sufficiently audible to banish any suspicion of loneliness.

I was raising my battery on to the table, and was connecting the wires carefully so as to explode the charge, when I heard a short, quick step outside the window, and immediately afterwards a loud knock at the outer door.

Now I very seldom had a call from any of my limited number of acquaintances, and certainly never upon such a night as this. I was astonished for a moment; then concluding that it was a visitor of Gretchen's, I continued to work at my apparatus.

To my very great surprise, after Gretchen had opened the door there was some muttering in the hall, and then a quiet tap at the entrance of my sanctum, followed by the appearance of a tall lady whom I could vow that I had never seen in my life before.

Her face was covered by a thick dark veil, and her dress was of the same sombre colour, so that I concluded her to be a widow. She walked in with a decisive energetic step, and after glancing round, seated herself quietly upon the sofa between the voltaic pile and my stand of reagents — all this without saying a word, or apparently taking the slightest notice of my presence.

"Good evening, madam," I remarked, when I had somewhat recovered my composure.

"Would you do me a favour, doctor?" she replied, brusquely, in a harsh voice, which harmonised with her gaunt angular figure.

"Surely, madam," I answered, in my most elegant manner. I remember a girl at Heidelberg used to say that I had a very fascinating way sometimes. Of course it was only in joke, but still something must have put it into her head or she would never have said it. "What can I do for you?" I asked.

"You can send away that servant of yours, who is listening at the door."

At this moment, before I could move hand or foot, there were a succession of tremendous bumps, followed by a terrible crash and a prolonged scream. It was evident that my unhappy domestic had fallen downstairs in her attempt to avoid detection. I was about to rise, but the stranger arrested me.

"Never mind now," she said. "We can proceed to business."

I bowed my head to show that I was all attention.

"The fact is, doctor," she continued, "that I wish you to come back with me and give me your opinion upon a case."

"My dear madam," I answered, "I have long retired from the practice of my profession. If you go down the street, however, you will see the surgery of Dr Benger, who is a most competent man, and who will be happy to accompany you."

"No, no," cried my companion, in great distress. "You or no one! You or no one! My poor dear husband cried out as I left him that Otto von Spee was the only man who could bring him back from the tomb. They will all be broken-hearted if I return without you. Besides, the professors at the hospital said that you were the only one in Europe who would be capable of dealing with it."

Now, devoted as I was to scientific research, I had always had a conviction in my mind that I had the makings in me of a first-class practical physician. It was inexpressibly consoling to hear that the heads of the profession had endorsed this opinion by referring a curious case to my judgment. The more I thought of it, however, the more extraordinary did it seem.

"Are you sure?" I asked.

"Oh yes, quite sure."

"But I am a specialist — a student of explosives. I have had very little experience in practice. What is the matter with your husband?"

"He has a tumour."

"A tumour? I know nothing of tumours."

"Oh come, dear Doctor von Spee; come and look at it!" implored the female, producing a handkerchief from her pocket and beginning to sob convulsively.

It was too much. I had lived a secluded life, and had never before seen a female in distress.

"Madam," I said, "I shall be happy to accompany you."

I regretted that promise the moment it was uttered. There was a wild howl of wind in the chimney which reminded me of the inclemency of the night. However, my word was pledged, and there was no possibility of escape. I left the room with as cheerful an aspect as possible, while Gretchen wrapped a shawl round my neck and muffled me up to the best of her ability.

What could there be about this tumour, I wondered, which had induced the learned surgeons to refer it to my judgment — I who was rather an artillerist than a physician? Could it be that the growth was of such stony hardness that no knife could remove it, and that explosives were necessary for its extraction? The idea was so comical that I could scarce refrain from laughing.

"Now, madam," I said, re-entering the study, "I am at your disposal." As I spoke I knocked against the electric machine, causing a slight transmission of the current along the wires, so that the submarine mine exploded with a crash, blowing a little column of water into the air. Accustomed as I was to such accidents, I confess that I was considerably started by the suddenness of the occurrence. My companion, however, sat perfectly impassive upon the sofa, and then rose without the slightest sign of surprise or emotion, and walked out of the room.

"She has the nerves of a grenadier," I mentally ejaculated, as I followed her into the street.

"Is it far?" I asked, as we started off through the storm.

"Not very far," she answered; "and I took the liberty of bringing a cab for you, for fear Herr Doctor might catch cold. Ah, here it comes."

As she spoke, a closed carriage dashed along the road, and pulled up beside us.

III

"Have you got Otto von Spee?" asked a sallow-faced man, letting down the window and protruding his head.

"Yes, here he is."

"Then shove him in."

For the moment I was inclined to regard the expression as a playful figure of speech, but my companion soon dispelled the delusion by seizing me by the collar and hurling me, with what seemed superhuman strength, into the vehicle. I fell upon the floor, and was dragged on to a seat by the man, while the other sprang in, slammed the door, and the horses dashed off at a furious gallop.

I lay back in a state of bewilderment, hardly able to realise what had occurred. It was pitch dark inside the carriage, but I could hear my two companions conversing in low whispers. Once I attempted to expostulate and demand an explanation of their conduct, but a threatening growl, and a rough hand placed over my mouth, warned me to be silent. I was neither a wealthy man nor particularly well connected, nor was I a politician. What, then, could be the object of these people in kidnapping me in such a elaborate fashion? The more I pondered over it, the more mysterious did it seem.

Once we halted for a moment, and a third man got into the carriage, who also inquired anxiously whether Otto von Spee had been secured, and expressed his satisfaction on being answered in the affirmative. After this stoppage we rattled along even more quickly than before, the vehicle rocking from side to side with its velocity, and the clatter of the horses' hoofs sounding above the howling of the gale. It seemed to me that we must have passed through every street in Berlin before, with a sudden jar, the coachman pulled up, and my captors intimated that I was to descend.

I had hardly time to look about me and realise the fact that I was in a narrow street in some low quarter of the city. A door opened in front of us, and the two men led me through it, while the herculean female followed us, effectually cutting off any hopes of escape.

We were in a long passage or corridor, feebly illuminated by a couple of flickering lamps, whose yellow glare seemed to intensify the darkness around them. After walking about twenty metres or more we came to a massive door, blocking our passage. One of my guardians struck it a blow with a stick which he carried in his hand, when it reverberated with a metallic clang, and swung open, closing with a snap behind us.

At this point I ventured to stop and expostulate with my companions once again. My only answer, however, was a shove from the individual behind me, which shot me through a half-opened door into a comfortable little chamber beyond. My captors followed in a more leisurely manner, and after turning the lock, they proceeded to seat themselves, motioning to me that I should do the same.

The room in which I found myself was small, but elegantly furnished. A fire was sparkling in the grate, and the bright colours of the handsome suite of furniture and variegated carpet helped to give it a cheering aspect. The pictures on the walls, however, went far towards neutralising this effect. They were very numerous, but every one of them treated of some unpleasant or murderous passage of history. Many of them were so distant that I was unable to decipher the inscription. To a scholar like myself, however, the majority were able to tell their own story. There was the lunatic Schtaps in the garden, making his attempt upon the life of the First Napoleon. Above it was a sketch of Orsini with his cowardly bomb, waiting silently among the loungers at the opera. A statuette of Ravaillac was placed upon a pedestal in the corner, while a large oil-painting of the strangling of the unhappy Emperor Paul in his bedchamber occupied the whole of one wall of the apartment.

These things did not tend to raise my spirits, and the appearance of my three companions was still less calculated to do so. I had several times doubted the sex of the individual who had seduced me from my comfortable home, but the veil had now been removed and revealed a dark moustache and sunburnt countenance, with a pair of searching, sinister eyes, which seemed to look into my very soul. Of the others, one was gaunt and cadaverous, the other insignificant-looking, with a straggling beard and unhealthy complexion.

"We are very sorry, Doctor von Spee, to be reduced to this necessity," said the last-mentioned individual, "but unhappily we had no other method of securing the pleasure of your society."

I bowed — a little sulkily, I am afraid.

"I must apologise for any little liberties I have taken, above all for having deprived you of the satisfaction of beholding my husband's remarkable tumour," said my original acquaintance.

I thought of the manner in which he had bundled me about like an empty portmanteau, and my bow was even more sulky than before.

"I trust, gentlemen," I remarked, "that since your practical joke has been so admirably carried out, you will now permit me to return to the studies which you have interrupted."

"Not so fast, Herr Doctor — not so fast," said the tall man, rising to his feet. "We have a little duty which you shall perform before you leave us. It is nothing more nor less than to give a few inquirers into truth a lesson upon your own special subject. Might I beg you to step in this direction?"

He walked over to a side door, painted of the same colour as the paper on the wall, and held it persuasively open. Resistance was useless, as the other confederates had also risen, and were standing on either side of me. I yielded to circumstances, and walked out as directed.

We passed down a second passage, rather shorter than the first, and much more brilliantly illuminated. At the end of it a heavy velvet curtain was hung, which covered a green baize folding-door. This was swung open, and I found myself, to my astonishment, in a large room in which a considerable number of people were assembled. They were arranged in long rows, and sat so as to face a raised platform at one end of the apartment, on which was a single chair, with a small round table, littered with a number of objects.

My companions ushered me in, and our entrance was greeted with considerable applause. It was clear that we had been awaited, for there was a general movement of expectation throughout the assembly. Glancing round, I could see that the majority of the company were dressed as artisans or labourers. There were some, however, who were respectably and even fashionably attired, and a few whose blue coats and gilt shoulder-bands proclaimed them to be officers in the army. Their nationalities seemed almost as varied as their occupations. I could distinguish the dolicho-cephalic head of the Teuton, the round, curl-covered cranium of the Celt, and the prognathous jaw and savage features of the Sclav. I could almost have imagined myself looking into one of the cabinets of casts in my friend Landerstein's anthropological museum.

However, I had not much time for wonder or reflection. One of my guardians led me across the room, and I found myself standing at the table, which I have already mentioned as being situated upon a raised dais. My appearance in this situation was the signal for a fresh outburst of applause, which, with clapping of hands and drumming of sticks upon the floor, lasted for some considerable time.

When it had subsided, the gaunt man who had come with me in the carriage walked up to the dais and addressed a few words to the audience. "Gentlemen," he said, "you will perceive that the committee have succeeded in keeping their promise and of bringing the celebrated—("beruhmte" was

the word he used)—Doctor Otto von Spee to address you."
Here there was renewed applause.

"Doctor," he continued, turning to me, "I think a few
words of public explanation will not be amiss in this matter.
You are well known as an authority upon explosives. Now
all these gentlemen and myself have an interest in this
subject, and would gladly listen to your views upon it. We
are particularly anxious that you should give us clear and
precise directions as to the method of preparing dynamite,
guncotton, and other such substances, as we sometimes have
a little difficulty in obtaining such things for our
experiments. You shall also tell us about the effect of
temperature, water, and other agents upon these substances,
the best method of storing them, and the way of using them
to the greatest advantage. For our part, we shall listen
attentively and treat you well, always provided that you
make no attempt to summon aid or to escape. Should you be
so ill-advised as to do either" — here he slapped his jacket
pocket — "you shall become as intimately acquainted with
projectiles as you now are with explosives." I cannot say
that this struck me as a good joke, but it seemed to meet
considerable favour among the audience.

"I wish to add a few words to the remarks of our learned
president," said a small man, rising up from among the first
line of the company. "I have placed upon the table such
materials as I could lay my hands upon in order that the
learned doctor may be able to illustrate his discourse by any
experiments which he may think appropriate. I may warn
him, in conclusion, to speak somewhat slowly and distinctly,
as some of his hearers are but imperfectly acquainted with
the German language."

Here was my old luck again with a vengeance! At a time
when Walderich and every gay dog in Berlin were snoring
peacefully in their beds, I — I, Doctor Otto von Spee, the
modest man of science, was lecturing to a murderous secret
organisation — for my audience could be nothing else — and

teaching them to forge the weapons with which they were to attack society and everything which should be treasured and revered. And on such a night as this too! Should I, then, put it in their power to convert a house into an arsenal, to destroy the stability of the Fatherland, and even perhaps attempt the life of my beloved kaiser? Never! I swore it — never!

Most small men who wear spectacles are obstinate. I am a small man with spectacles, and I was no exception to the rule. I clenched my teeth, and felt that, *ruat cœlum*, never a word should pass my lips that might be of any help to them. I should not refuse to lecture, but I was determined to avoid those very points upon which they desired to be instructed.

I was not allowed much time for meditation. An ominous murmur among the audience, and a shuffling of feet upon the floor, betokened their impatience. I must say, however, that many of them seemed actuated with rather kindly feelings towards me, more particularly one stoutish individual of a well-marked Celtic type, who, not content with smiling all over his florid countenance, waves his arms occasionally in motions intended to indicate sympathy and inspire confidence.

I stepped up to the table, which was covered all over with such objects as were thought to have a bearing upon my subject. Some of them were rather curious — a lump of salt, an iron teapot, part of the broken axle of a wheel, and a large pair of kitchen bellows. Others were more appropriate. There was a piece of guncotton which could not have weighed less than a couple of pounds, coarse cotton, starch, various acids, a Bunsen burner, tubes of fulminate of mercury, some dynamite powder, and a large pitcher of water. There was also a caraffe and tumbler for my own use, should I feel so disposed.

"Meine herren," I began, with perhaps a slight quaver in my voice, "we have met here tonight for the purpose of studying dynamite and other explosives." It flowed naturally from my lips, as it was the stereotyped formula with which my discourses at the Educationische Institut were usually commenced. My audience seemed, however, to be much amused, and the florid Celt was convulsed with admiration and merriment. Even the forbidding-looking man who had been referred to as the president condescended to smile his approval and remark that I adapted myself readily to my circumstances.

"These substances," I continued, "are powerful agents either for good or for evil. For good when used for the quarrying of rocks, the removal of impediments to navigation, or the destruction of houses during a conflagration. For evil—"

"I think you had better pass on to something more practical," said the president, grimly.

"On dipping starch into certain liquids," I resumed, "it is found to assume an explosive property. The attention of a learned countryman of ours, the chemist Schönbein, was directed to the fact, and he found that by treating cotton in a similar manner the effect was enormously increased. Schönbien was a man respected among his contemporaries, devoted to his country, and loyal—"

"Pass on!" said the president.

"After being treated in this fashion," I continued, "the cotton is found to gain eighty per cent in weight. This substance is more susceptible to an increase of temperature than gunpowder, igniting at 300 degrees Fahrenheit, while the latter requires a heat of 560 degrees for its explosion. Guncotton can also be exploded by a blow, which is not the case with a mixture of carbon, sulphur, and saltpetre."

Here there were some angry murmurs among the company, and the president interrupted me for the third time.

"These gentlemen complain," he said, "that you have left no definite impression upon their minds as to how the substance is manufactured. Perhaps you will kindly dwell more fully upon the point."

"I have no further remarks to make," I said.

There was another threatening murmur, and the president took something out of the pocket of his coat, and toyed with it negligently. "I think you had better reconsider your decision," he remarked.

Most little men with spectacles are timid. Again I was no exception to the rule. I am ashamed to say that the peril of my Fatherland and even of my kaiser suddenly vanished from my recollection. I only realised that I, Otto von Spee, was standing upon the brink of eternity. After all, I argued, they could find out for themselves in any book upon chemistry. Why should my valuable life be sacrificed for such a trifle? I resumed my lecture with somewhat undignified haste.

"Guncotton is manufactured by steeping cotton waste in nitric acid. The explosion is caused by the oxygen of the acid combining with the carbon of the wool. It should be well cleaned with water after manufacture, otherwise the superfluous nitric acid acts directly upon the wool, charring it and gradually reducing it to a gummy mass. During this process heat is often evolved sufficient to explode the cotton, so that it is a dangerous matter to neglect the cleaning. After this a little sulphuric acid may be used to get rid of the moisture, when the substance is ready for use."

There was considerable applause at this point of my discourse, several of the audience taking notes of my remarks.

While I had been speaking I had been making a careful survey of the room in the hope of seeing some possibility of escape. The dais upon which I stood extended as far as the side wall, in which there was a window. The window was half open, and, could I reach it, there appeared to be a deserted-looking garden outside, which might communicate with the street. No one could intercept me before I reached the window, but then there was the deadly weapon with which my cadaverous acquaintance was still trifling. He was sitting on the other side, and the table would partially protect me should I venture upon a dash. Could I screw up my courage to make the attempt? Not yet, at any rate.

"General von Link," I continued, "the Austrian artillerist, is one of our leading authorities upon guncotton. He experimented upon it in field-pieces, but—"

"Never mind that," said the president.

"After being manufactured, guncotton may be compressed under water. When compressed it is perfectly safe, and cannot be discharged. This sample which we have upon the table is not compressed. No amount of heat will have any effect upon the wet cotton. In an experiment tried in England a storehouse containing guncotton was burned down without there being any explosion. If, however, a charge of fulminated mercury, or a small piece of dry cotton, be fired in connection with a damp disc, it will be sufficient to discharge it. I shall now proceed to demonstrate this to you by an experiment."

An idea had come into my mind. Upon the table there was lying a mixture of sugar and chlorate of potash, used with sulphuric acid as a fuse for mining purposes. A bottle of the acid was also ready to my hand. I knew the white dense cloud of smoke which is raised by the imperfect combustion of these bodies. Could I make it serve as a screen between the weapon of the president and myself?

For a moment the plan seemed wild and unfeasible; still, it offered some chance of escape, and the more I thought it over the more reconciled I became to it. Of course, even after getting through the window there was the possibility that the garden might prove to be a *cul-de-sac*, and that my pursuers might overtake me. But then, on the other hand, I had no guarantee that I might not be murdered at the conclusion of my lecture. From what I knew of the habits of such men I considered it to be extremely probable. It was better to risk — but no, I would not think of what I was risking.

"I am now going to show you the effect of fulminate of

mercury upon a small piece of damp cotton," I said, shaking out the sugar and chlorate of potash upon the edge of the table and pushing the large piece of cotton to the other end to be out of danger from the effects of the explosion. "You will observe that the fact of the substance having been soaked with water does not in any way hinder its action." Here I poured the sulphuric acid over the mixture, dropped the bottle, and fled for the window amid a perfect cloud of smoke.

Most little men with spectacles are not remarkable for activity. Ha! there at last I proved myself to be an exception. I seemed hardly to put my foot to the ground between leaving the table and shooting out through the window as the equestrians fly through hoops in the circus. I was well outside before the sharp crack which I was expecting sounded in the chamber behind me, and then—

Ah! what then? How can I ever hope to describe it? There was a low, deep rumble, which seemed to shake the ground, swelling and swelling in sound until it culminated in a roar which split the very heavens. Flames danced before my eyes, burning wood and stones and *débris* came clattering down around me, and as I stared about in bewilderment I received a crushing blow upon the head, and fell.

* * * * *

How long I may have remained unconscious it is difficult to say. Some time, at any rate, for when I came to myself I was stretched upon the bed in my own little chamber at home, while the devoted Gretchen bathed my temples with vinegar and water. In the doorway were standing a couple of stalwart *polizei diener*, who bobbed their helmeted heads and grinned their satisfaction on seeing that I was returning to consciousness.

It was some while before I could recall anything of what had passed. Then gradually came the recollection of my mysterious visitor, of the wild drive through the storm, of the impromptu lecture on dynamite, and lastly of some strange and unaccountable accident. Strange it still remains, but I think that when we reflect that the table was between the bullet and me, and that on the table were two pounds of guncotton liable to ignition at a blow, we have not very far to go for an explanation. I have fired a pistol at a distance into a small piece of the same substance since that occasion with very much the same result.

And where was the house? you will ask, and what was the fate of its inmates? Ah! there my lips are sealed. The police of the Fatherland are active and cunning, and they have commanded me to say nothing — not even to my dearest friend — upon either point. No doubt they have their reasons for it, and I must obey. Perhaps they wish other conspirators to imagine that more has been found out than is actually the case. I may say, however, that it is not conducive to long life or perfect health to be present on such an occasion. That, at least, no once can object to.

I am nearly well again now, thanks to Gretchen and to Dr Benger, who lives down the road. I can hobble about, and my neighbours are already beginning to complain of the noxious vapours which I evolve. I fear I have not quite the same enthusiasm, however, upon the subject of explosives as I entertained before my midnight lecture on dynamite. The subject seems to have lost many of its charms. It may be that in the course of time I may return to my first love once again; at present, however, I remain a quiet *privat docent* of the more elementary branches of chemistry. It is that very quietness which weighs upon my mind. I fear that I am on the verge of some other unexpected adventure. There is one thing, however, upon which I am unalterably determined. Should every relative that I have in the world, with the Imperial family and half the population of Berlin, be clamouring at my door for medical advice, I shall never again protrude my head after nightfall. I am content to work away in my own

little groove, and have laid aside for ever the pretensions to
be looked upon as a practical physician which I entertained
before that eventful Christmas Eve.

P. G. Wodehouse

SUNDERED HEARTS

IN the smoking-room of the club-house a cheerful fire was burning, and the Oldest Member glanced from time to time out of the window into the gathering dusk. Snow was falling lightly on the links. From where he sat, the Oldest Member had a good view of the ninth green; and presently, out of the greyness of the December evening, there appeared over the brow of the hill a golf-ball. It trickled across the green and stopped within a yard of the hole. The Oldest Member nodded approvingly. A good approach-shot.

A young man in a tweed suit clambered on to the green, holed out with easy confidence, and, shouldering his bag, made his way to the club-house. A few moments later he entered the smoking-room, and uttered an exclamation of rapture at the sight of the fire.

"I'm frozen stiff!"

He rang for a waiter and ordered a hot drink. The Oldest Member gave a gracious assent to the suggestion that he should join him.

"I like playing in winter," said the young man. "You get the course to yourself, for the world is full of slackers who only turn out when the weather suits them. I cannot understand where they get the nerve to call themselves golfers."

"Not everyone is as keen as you are, my boy," said the Sage, dipping gratefully into his hot drink. "If they were, the world would be a better place, and we should hear less of all this modern unrest."

"I *am* pretty keen," admitted the young man.

"I have only encountered one man whom I could describe as keener. I allude to Mortimer Sturgis."

"The fellow who took up golf at thirty-eight and let the girl he was engaged to marry go off with someone else because he hadn't the time to combine golf with courtship? I remember. You were telling me about him the other day."

"There is a sequel to that story, if you would care to hear it," said the Oldest Member.

"You have the honour," said the young man. "Go ahead!"

Some people (began the Oldest Member) considered that Mortimer Sturgis was too wrapped up in golf, and blamed him for it. I could never see eye to eye with them. In the days of King Arthur nobody thought the worse of a young knight if he suspended all his social and business engagements in favour of a search for the Holy Grail. In the Middle Ages a man could devote his whole life to the Crusades, and the public fawned upon him. Why, then, blame the man of today for a zealous attention to the modern equivalent, the Quest of Scratch! Mortimer Sturgis never became a scratch player, but he did eventually get his handicap down to nine, and I honour him for it.

The story which I am about to tell begins in what might be called the middle period of Sturgis's career. He had reached the stage when his handicap was a wobbly twelve; and, as you are no doubt aware, it is then that a man really begins to golf in the true sense of the word. Mortimer's fondness for the game until then had been merely tepid compared with what it became now. He had played a little before, but now he really buckled to and got down to it. It was at this point, too, that he began once more to entertain thoughts of marriage. A profound statistician in this one department, he had discovered that practically all the finest exponents of the

art are married men; and the thought that there might be
something in the holy state which improved a man's game,
and that he was missing a good thing, troubled him a great
deal. Moreover, the paternal instinct had awakened in him.
As he justly pointed out, whether marriage improved your
game or not, it was to Old Tom Morris's marriage that the
existence of young Tommy Morris, winner of the British
Open Championship four times in succession, could be
directly traced. In fact, at the age of forty-two, Mortimer
Sturgis was in just the frame of mind to take some nice girl
aside and ask her to become a stepmother to his eleven
drivers, his baffy, his twenty-eight putters, and the rest of
the ninety-four clubs which he had accumulated in the
course of his golfing career. The sole stipulation, of course,
which he made when dreaming his day-dreams was that the
future Mrs Sturgis must be a golfer. I can still recall the
horror in his face when one girl, admirable in other respects,
said the she had never heard of Harry Vardon, and didn't he
mean Dolly Vardon? She has since proved an excellent wife
and mother, but Mortimer Sturgis never spoke to her again.

With the coming of January, it was Mortimer's practice
to leave England and go to the South of France, where there
was sunshine and crisp dry turf. He pursued his usual custom
this year. With his suitcase and his ninety-four clubs he went
off to Saint Brüle, staying as he always did at the Hôtel
Superbe, where they knew him, and treated with an amiable
tolerance his habit of practising chip-shots in his bedroom.
On the first evening, after breaking a statuette of the Infant
Samuel in Prayer, he dressed and went down to dinner. And
the first thing he was was Her.

Mortimer Sturgis, as you know, had been engaged before,
but Betty Weston had never inspired the tumultuous rush of
emotion which the mere sight of this girl set loose in him. He
told me later that just to watch her holing out her soup gave
him a sort of feeling you get when your drive collides with a
rock in the middle of a tangle of rough and kicks back into
the middle of the fairway. If golf had come late in life to

Mortimer Sturgis, love came later still, and just as the golf, attacking him in middle life, had been some golf, so was the love considerable love. Mortimer finished his dinner in a trance, which is the best way to do it at some hotels, and then scoured the place for someone who would introduce him. He found such a person eventually and the meeting took place.

She was a small and rather fragile-looking girl, with big blue eyes and a cloud of golden hair. She had a sweet expression, and her left wrist was in a sling. She looked up at Mortimer as if she had at last found something that amounted to something. I am inclined to think it was a case of love at first sight on both sides.

"Fine weather we're having," said Mortimer, who was a capital conversationalist.

"Yes," said the girl.

"I like fine weather."

"So do I."

"There's something about fine weather!"

"Yes."

"It's — it's — well, fine weather's so much finer than weather that isn't fine," said Mortimer.

He looked at the girl a little anxiously, fearing he might be taking her out of her depth, but she seemed to have followed his train of thought perfectly.

"Yes, isn't it?" she said. "It's so — so fine."

"That's just what I meant," said Mortimer. "So fine. You've just hit it."

He was charmed. The combination of beauty with intelligence is so rare.

"I see you've hurt your wrist," he went on, pointing to the sling.

"Yes. I strained it a little playing in the championship."

"The championship?" Mortimer was interested. "It's awfully rude of me," he said, apologetically, "but I didn't catch your name just now."

"My name is Somerset."

Mortimer had been bending forward solicitously. He overbalanced and nearly fell off his chair. The shock had been stunning. Even before he had met and spoken to her, he had told himself that he loved this girl with the stored-up love of a lifetime. And she was Mary Somerset! The hotel lobby danced before Mortimer's eyes.

The name will, of course, be familiar to you. In the early rounds of the Ladies' Open Golf Championship of that year nobody had paid much attention to Mary Somerset. She had survived her first two matches, but her opponents had been nonentities like herself. And then, in the third round, she had met and defeated the champion. From that point on, her name was on everybody's lips. She became favourite. And she justified the public confidence by sailing into the final and winning easily. And here she was, talking to him like an ordinary person, and, if he could read the message in her eyes, not altogether indifferent to his charms, if you could call them that.

"Golly!" said Mortimer, awed.

Their friendship ripened rapidly, as friendships do in the South of France. In that favoured clime, you find the girl and Nature does the rest. On the second morning of their acquaintance Mortimer invited her to walk round the links with him and watch him play. He did it a little diffidently, for his golf was not of the calibre that would be likely to extort admiration from a champion. On the other hand, one should never let slip the opportunity of acquiring wrinkles on the game, and he thought that Miss Somerset, if she watched one or two of his shots, might tell him just what he ought to do. And sure enough, the opening arrived on the fourth hole, where Mortimer, after a drive which surprised even him, found his ball in a nasty cuppy lie.

He turned to the girl.

"What ought I to do here?" he asked.

Miss Somerset looked at the ball. She seemed to be weighing the matter in her mind.

"Give it a good hard knock," she said.

Mortimer knew what she meant. She was advocating a full iron. The only trouble was that, when he tried anything more ambitious than a half-swing, except off the tee, he almost invariably topped. However, he could not fail this wonderful girl, so he swung well back and took a chance. His enterprise was rewarded. The ball flew out of the indentation in the turf as cleanly as though John Henry Taylor had been behind it, and rolled, looking neither to left nor to right, straight for the pin. A few moments later Mortimer Sturgis had holed out one under bogey, and it was only the fear that, having known him for so short a time, she might be startled and refuse him that kept him from proposing then and there. This exhibition of golfing general-ship on her part had removed his last doubts. He knew that, if he lived for ever, there could be no other girl in the world for him. With her at his side, what might he not do? He might get his handicap down to six — to three — to scratch — to plus something! Good heavens, why, even the Amateur Championship was not outside the range of possibility. Mortimer Sturgis shook his putter solemnly in the air, and vowed a silent vow that he would win this pearl among women.

Now, when a man feels like that, it is impossible to restrain him long. For a week Mortimer Sturgis's soul sizzled within him: then he could contain himself no longer. One night, at one of the informal dances at the hotel, he drew the girl out on to the moonlit terrace.

"Miss Somerset——" he began, stuttering with emotion like an imperfectly-corked bottle of ginger-beer. "Miss Somerset — may I call you Mary?"

The girl looked at him with eyes that shone softly in the dim light.

"Mary?" she repeated. "Why, of course, if you like——"

"If I like!" cried Mortimer. "Don't you know that it is my dearest wish? Don't you know that I would rather be permitted to call you Mary than do the first hole at Muirfield in two? Oh, Mary, how I have longed for this moment! I love you! I love you! Ever since I met you I have known that you were the one girl in this vast world whom I would die to win! Mary, will you be mine? Shall we go round together? Will you fix up a match with me on the links of life which shall end only when the Grim Reaper lays us both a stymie?"

She drooped towards him.

"Mortimer!" she murmured.

He held out his arms, then drew back. His face had grown suddenly tense, and there were lines of pain about his mouth.

"Wait!" he said, in a strained voice. "Mary, I love you dearly, and because I love you so dearly I cannot let you trust your sweet life to me blindly. I have a confession to make. I am not — I have not always been" — he paused — "a good man," he said, in a low voice.

She started indignantly.

"How can you say that? You are the best, the kindest, the bravest man I have ever met! Who but a good man would have risked his life to save me from drowning?"

"Drowning?" Mortimer's voice seemed perplexed. "You? What do you mean?"

"Have you forgotten the time when I fell in the sea last week, and you jumped in with all your clothes on——"

"Of course, yes," said Mortimer. "I remember now. It was the day I did the long seventh in five. I got off a good tee-shot straight down the fairway, took a baffy for my second, and—— But that is not the point. It is sweet and generous of you to think so highly of what was the merest commonplace act of ordinary politeness, but I must repeat, that judged by the standards of your snowy purity, I am not a good man. I do not come to you clean and spotless as a young girl should expect her husband to come to her. Once, playing in a foursome, my ball fell in some long grass. Nobody was near me. We had no caddies, and the others were on the fairway. God knows——" His voice shook. "God knows, I struggled against the temptation. But I fell. I kicked the ball on to a little bare mound, from which it was an easy task with a nice half-mashie to reach the green for a snappy seven. Mary, there have been times when, going round by myself, I have allowed myself ten-foot putts on three holes in succession, simply in order to be able to say I had done the course in under a hundred. Ah, you shrink from me! You are disgusted!"

"I'm not disgusted! And I don't shrink! I only shivered because it is rather cold."

"Then you can love me in spite of my past?"

"Mortimer!"

She fell into his arms.

"My dearest," he said presently, "what a happy life ours will be. That is, if you do not find that you have made a mistake."

"A mistake!" she cried, scornfully.

"Well, my handicap is twelve, you know, and not so darned twelve at that. There are days when I play my second from the fairway of the next hole but one, days when I couldn't putt into a coal-hole with 'Welcome!' written over it. And you are a Ladies' Open Champion. Still, if you think it's all right——. Oh, Mary, you little know how I have dreamed of some day marrying a really first-class golfer! Yes, that was my vision — of walking up the aisle with some sweet plus two girl on my arm. You shivered again. You are catching cold."

"It is a little cold," said the girl. She spoke in a small voice.

"Let me take you in, sweetheart," said Mortimer. "I'll just put you in a comfortable chair with a nice cup of coffee, and then I think I really must come out again and tramp about and think how perfectly splendid everything is."

They were married a few weeks later, very quietly, in the little village church of Saint Brûle. The secretary of the local golf-club acted as best man for Mortimer, and a girl from the hotel was the only bridesmaid. The whole business was rather a disappointment to Mortimer, who had planned out a somewhat florid ceremony at St. George's, Hanover Square, with the Vicar of Tooting (a scratch player excellent at short approach shots) officiating, and "The Voice That Breathed O'er St. Andrews" booming from the organ. He had even had the idea of copying the military wedding and escorting his bride out of the church under an arch of crossed cleeks. But she would have none of this pomp. She insisted on a quiet wedding, and for the honeymoon trip preferred a tour through Italy. Mortimer, who had wanted to go to Scotland to visit the birthplace of James Braid, yielded amiably, for he loved her dearly. But he did not think much of Italy. In Rome, the great monuments of the past left him cold. Of the Temples of Vespasian, all he thought was that it would be a devil of a place to be bunkered behind. The Colosseum aroused a faint spark of interest in him, as he speculated whether Abe Mitchell would use a full brassey to carry it. In Florence, the view over the Tuscan Hills from the Terre Rosa, Fiesole, over which his bride waxed enthusiastic, seemed to him merely a nasty bit of rough which would take a deal of getting out of.

And so, in the fullness of time, they came home to Mortimer's cosy little house adjoining the links.

Mortimer was so busy polishing his ninety-four clubs on the evening of their arrival that he failed to notice that his wife was preoccupied. A less busy man would have perceived at a glance that she was distinctly nervous. She started at sudden noises, and once, when he tried the newest of his mashie-niblicks and broke one of the drawing-room windows, she screamed sharply. In short her manner was strange, and, if Edgar Allan Poe had put her into "The Fall of the House of Usher", she would have fitted it like the paper on the wall. She had the air of one waiting tensely for the approach of some imminent doom. Mortimer, humming gaily to himself as he sand-papered the blade of his twenty-second putter, observed nothing of this. He was thinking of the morrow's play.

"Your wrist's quite well again now, darling, isn't it?" he said.

"Yes. Yes, quite well."

"Fine!" said Mortimer. "We'll breakfast early — say at half-past seven — and then we'll be able to get in a couple of rounds before lunch. A couple more in the afternoon will about see us through. One doesn't want to over-golf oneself the first day." He swung the putter joyfully. "How had we better play do you think? We might start with you giving me a half."

She did not speak. She was very pale. She clutched the arm of her chair tightly till the knuckles showed white under the skin.

To anybody but Mortimer her nervousness would have been even more obvious on the following morning, as they reached the first tee. Her eyes were dull and heavy, and she started when a grasshopper chirruped. But Mortimer was too occupied with thinking how jolly it was having the course to themselves to notice anything.

He scooped some sand out of the box, and took a ball out of her bag. His wedding present to her had been a brand-new golf-bag, six dozen balls, and a full set of the most expensive clubs, all born in Scotland.

"Do you like a high tee?" he asked.

"Oh, no," she replied, coming with a start out of her thoughts. "Doctors say it's indigestible."

Mortimer laughed merrily.

"Deuced good!" he chuckled. "Is that your own or did you read it in a comic paper? There you are!" He placed the ball on a little hill of sand, and got up. "Now let's see some of that championship form of yours!"

She burst into tears.

"My darling!"

Mortimer ran to her and put his arms round her. She tried weakly to push him away.

"My angel! What is it?"

She sobbed brokenly. Then, with an effort, she spoke.

"Mortimer, I have deceived you!"

"Deceived me?"

"I have never played golf in my life! I don't even know how to hold the caddie!"

Mortimer's heart stood still. This sounded like the gibberings of an unbalanced mind, and no man likes his wife to begin gibbering immediately after the honeymoon.

"My precious! You are not yourself!"

"I am! that's the whole trouble. I'm myself and not the girl you thought I was!"

Mortimer stared at her, puzzled. He was thinking that it was a little difficult and that, to work it out properly, he would need a pencil and a bit of paper.

"My name is not Mary!"

"But you said it was."

"I didn't. You asked if you could call me Mary, and I said you might, because I loved you too much to deny your smallest whim. I was going on to say that it wasn't my name, but you interrupted me."

"Not Mary!" The horrid truth was coming home to Mortimer. "You were not Mary Somerset?"

"Mary is my cousin. My name is Mabel."

"But you said you had sprained your wrist playing in the championship."

"So I had. The mallet slipped in my hand."

"The mallet!" Mortimer clutched at his forehead. "You didn't say 'the mallet'?"

"Yes, Mortimer! The mallet!"

A faint blush of shame mantled her cheek, and into her blue eyes there came a look of pain, but she faced him bravely.

"I am the Ladies' Open Croquet Champion!" she whispered.

Mortimer Sturgis cried aloud, a cry that was like the shriek of some wounded animal.

"Croquet!" He gulped and stared at her with unseeing eyes. He was no prude, but he had those decent prejudices of which no self-respecting man can wholly rid himself, however broadminded he may try to be. "Croquet!"

There was a long silence. The light breeze sang in the pines above them. The grasshoppers chirruped at their feet.

She began to speak again in a low, monotonous voice.

"I blame myself! I should have told you before, while there was yet time for you to withdraw. I should have confessed this to you that night on the terrace in the moonlight. But you swept me off my feet, and I was in your arms before I realised what you would think of me. It was only then that I understood what my supposed skill at golf meant to you, and then it was too late. I loved you too much to let you go! I could not bear the thought of you recoiling from me. Oh, I was mad — mad! I knew that I could not keep up the deception forever, that you must find me out in time. But I had a wild hope that by then we should be so close to one another that you might find it in your heart to forgive. But I was wrong. I see it now. There are some things that no man can forgive. Some things," she repeated, dully, "which no man can forgive."

She turned away. Mortimer awoke from his trance.

"Stop!" he cried. "Don't go!"

"I must go."

"I want to talk this over."

She shook her head sadly and started to walk slowly across the sunlit grass. Mortimer watched her, his brain in a whirl of chaotic thoughts. She disappeared through the trees.

Mortimer sat down on the tee-box, and buried his face in his hands. For a time he could think of nothing but the cruel blow he had received. This was the end of those rainbow visions of himself and her going through life side by side, she lovingly criticising his stance and his back-swing, he learning wisdom from her. A croquet-player! He was married to a woman who hit coloured balls through hoops.

Mortimer Sturgis writhed in torment. A strong man's agony.

The mood passed. How long it had lasted, he did not know. But suddenly, as he sat there, he became once more aware of the glow of the sunshine and the singing of the birds. It was as if a shadow had lifted. Hope and optimism crept into his heart.

He loved her. He loved her still. She was part of him, and nothing that she could do had power to alter that. She had deceived him, yes. But why had she deceived him? Because she loved him so much that she could not bear to lose him. Dash it all, it was a bit of a compliment.

And, after all, poor girl, was it her fault? Was it not rather the fault of her upbringing? Probably she had been taught to play croquet when a mere child, hardly able to distinguish right from wrong. No steps had been taken to eradicate the virus from her system, and the thing had become chronic. Could she be blamed? Was she not more to be pitied than censured?

Mortimer rose to his feet, his heart swelling with generous forgiveness. The black horror had passed from him. The future seemed once more bright. It was not too late. She was still young, many years younger than he himself had been when he took up golf, and surely, if she put herself into the hands of a good specialist and practised every day, she might still hope to become a fair player. He reached the house and ran in, calling her name.

No answer came. He sped from room to room, but all were empty.

She had gone. The house was there. The furniture was there. The canary sang in its cage, the cook in the kitchen. The pictures still hung on the walls. But she had gone. Everything was at home except his wife.

Finally, propped up against the cup he had once won in a handicap competition, he saw a letter. With a sinking heart he tore open the envelope.

It was a pathetic, a tragic letter, the letter of a woman
endeavouring to express all the anguish of a torn heart with
one of those fountain-pens which suspend the flow of ink
about twice in every three words. The gist of it was that she
felt she had wronged him; that, though he might forgive, he
could never forget; and that she was going away, away out
into the world alone.

Mortimer sank into a chair, and stared blankly before him.
She had scratched the match.

I am not a married man myself, so have had no experience
of how it feels to have one's wife whiz off silently into the
unknown; but I should imagine that it must be something like
taking a full swing with a brassey and missing the ball.
Something, I take it, of the same sense of mingled shock,
chagrin, and the feeling that nobody loves one, which
attacks a man in such circumstances, must come to the
bereaved husband. And one can readily understand how
terribly the incident must have shaken Mortimer Sturgis. I
was away at the time, but I am told by those who saw him
that his game went all to pieces.

He had never shown much indication of becoming
anything in the nature of a first-class golfer, but he had
managed to acquire one or two decent shots. His work with
the light iron was not at all bad, and he was a fairly steady
putter. But now, under the shadow of this tragedy, he
dropped right back to the form of his earliest period. It was a
pitiful sight to see this gaunt, haggard man with the look of
dumb anguish behind his spectacles taking as many as three
shots sometimes to get past the ladies' tee. His slice, of which
he had almost cured himself, returned with such virulence
that in the list of ordinary hazards he had now to include the
tee-box. And, when he was not slicing, he was pulling. I
have heard that he was known, when driving at the sixth, to
get bunkered in his own caddie, who had taken up his
position directly behind him. As for the deep sand-trap in

front of the seventh green, he spent so much of his time in it that there was some informal talk among the members of the committee of charging him a small weekly rent.

A man of comfortable independent means, he lived during these days on next to nothing. Golf-balls cost him a certain amount, but the bulk of his income he spent in efforts to discover his wife's whereabouts. He advertised in all the papers. He employed private detectives. He even, much as it revolted his finer instincts, took to travelling about the country, watching croquet matches. But she was never among the players. I am not sure that he did not find a melancholy comfort in this, for it seemed to show that, whatever his wife might be and whatever she might be doing, she had not gone right under.

Summer passed. Autumn came and went. Winter arrived. The days grew bleak and chill, and an early fall of snow, heavier than had been known at that time of the year for a long while, put an end to golf. Mortimer spent his days indoors, staring gloomily through the window at the white mantle that covered the earth.

It was Christmas Eve.

The young man shifted uneasily on his seat. His face was long and sombre.

"All this is very depressing," he said.

"These soul tragedies," agreed the Oldest Member, "are never very cheery."

"Look here," said the young man, firmly, "tell me one thing frankly, as man to man. Did Mortimer find her dead in the snow, covered except for her face, on which still lingered that faint, sweet smile which he remembered so well? Because, if he did, I'm going home."

"No, no," protested the Oldest Member. "Nothing of that kind."

"You're sure? You aren't going to spring it on me suddenly?"

"No, no!"

The young man breathed a relieved sigh.

"It was your saying that about the white mantle covering the earth that made me suspicious."

The Sage resumed.

It was Christmas Eve. All day the snow had been falling, and now it lay thick and deep over the countryside. Mortimer Sturgis, his frugal dinner concluded — what with losing his wife and not being able to get any golf, he had little appetite these days — was sitting in his drawing-room, moodily polishing the blade of his jigger. Soon wearying of this once congenial task, he laid down the club and went to the front door to see if there was any chance of a thaw. But no. It was freezing. The snow, as he tested it with his shoe, crackled crisply. The sky above was black and full of cold stars. It seemed to Mortimer that the sooner he packed up and went to the South of France, the better. He was just about to close the door, when suddenly he thought he heard his own name called.

"Mortimer!"

Had he been mistaken? The voice had sounded faint and far away.

"Mortimer!"

He thrilled from head to foot. This time there could be no mistake. It was the voice he knew so well, his wife's voice, and it had come from somewhere down near the garden-gate. It is difficult to judge distance where sounds are concerned, but Mortimer estimated that the voice had spoken about a short mashie-niblick and an easy putt from where he stood.

The next moment he was racing down the snow-covered path. And then his heart stood still. What was that dark something on the ground just inside the gate? He leaped towards it. He passed his hands over it. It was a human body.

Quivering, he struck a match. It went out. He struck another. That went out, too. He struck a third, and it burnt with a steady flame; and, stooping, he saw that it was his wife who lay there, cold and stiff. Her eyes were closed, and on her face still lingered that faint, sweet smile which he remembered so well.

The young man rose with a set face. He reached for his golf-bag.

"I call that a dirty trick," he said, "after you promised—"

The Sage waved him back to his seat.

"Have no fear! She had only fainted."

"You said she was cold."

"Wouldn't you be cold if you were lying in the snow?"

"And stiff."

"Mrs Sturgis was stiff because the train-service was bad, it being the holiday season, and she had had to walk all the way from the junction, a distance of eight miles. Sit down and allow me to proceed."

Tenderly, reverently, Mortimer Sturgis picked her up and began to bear her into the house. Half-way there, his foot slipped on a piece of ice and he fell heavily, barking his shin and shooting his lovely burden out on to the snow.

The fall brought her to. She opened her eyes.

"Mortimer, darling!" she said.

Mortimer had just been going to say something else, but he checked himself.

"Are you alive?" he asked.

"Yes," she replied.

"Thank God!" said Mortimer, scooping some snow out of the back of his collar.

Together they went into the house, and into the drawing-room. Wife gazed at husband, husband at wife. There was a silence.

"Rotten weather!" said Mortimer.

"Yes, isn't it!"

The spell was broken. They fell into each other's arms. And presently they were sitting side by side on the sofa, holding hands, just as if that awful parting had been but a dream.

It was Mortimer who made the first reference to it.

"I say, you know," he said, "you oughtn't to have nipped away like that!"

"I thought you hated me!"

"Hated *you*! I love you better than life itself! I would sooner have smashed my pet driver than have had you leave me!"

She thrilled at the words.

"Darling!"

Mortimer fondled her hand.

"I was just coming back to tell you that I loved you still. I was going to suggest that you took lessons from some good professional. And I found you gone!"

"I wasn't worthy of you, Mortimer!"

"My angel!" He pressed his lips to her hair, and spoke solemnly. "All this has taught me a lesson, dearest. I knew all along, and I know it more than ever now, that it is you — you that I want. Just you! I don't care if you don't play golf. I don't care——" He hesitated, then went on manfully. "I don't care even if you play croquet, so long as you are with me!"

For a moment her face showed rapture that made it almost angelic. She uttered a low moan of ecstasy. She kissed him. Then she rose.

"Mortimer, look!"

"What at?"

"Me. Just look!"

The jigger which he had been polishing lay on a chair close by. She took it up. From the bowl of golf-balls on the mantelpiece she selected a brand-new one. She placed it on the carpet. She addressed it. Then, with a merry cry of

"Fore!" she drove it hard and straight through the glass of the china-cupboard.

"Good God!" cried Mortimer, astounded. It had been a bird of a shot.

She turned to him, her whole face alight with that beautiful smile.

"When I left you, Mortie," she said, "I had but one aim in life, somehow to make myself worthy of you. I saw your advertisements in the papers, and I longed to answer them, but I was not ready. All this long, weary while I have been in the village of Auchtermuchtie, in Scotland, studying under Tamms McMickle."

"Not the Tamms McMickle who finished fourth in the Open Championship of 1911, and had the best ball in the foursome in 1912 with Jock McHaggis, Andy McHeather, and Sandy McHoots!"

"Yes, Mortimer, the very same. Oh, it was difficult at first. I missed my mallet, and longed to steady the ball with my foot and use the toe of the club. Wherever there was a direction post I aimed at it automatically. But I conquered my weakness. I practised steadily. And now Mr McMickle says my handicap would be a good twenty-four on any links." She smiled apologetically. "Of course, that doesn't sound much to you! You were a twelve when I left you, and now I suppose you are down to eight or something."

Mortimer shook his head.

"Alas, no!" he replied, gravely. "My game went right off for some reason or other, and I'm twenty-four, too."

"For some reason or other!" She uttered a cry. "Oh, I know what the reason was! How can I ever forgive myself! I have ruined your game!"

The brightness came back to Mortimer's eyes. He embraced her fondly.

"Do not reproach yourself, dearest," he murmured. "It is the best thing that could have happened. From now on, we start level, two hearts that beat as one, two drivers that drive as one. I could not wish it otherwise. By George! It's just like that thing of Tennyson's."

He recited the lines softly:

> My bride,
> My wife, my life. Oh, we will walk the links
> Yoked in all exercise of noble end,
> And so thro' those dark bunkers off the course
> That no man knows. Indeed, I love thee: come,
> Yield thyself up: our handicaps are one;
> Accomplish thou my manhood and thyself;
> Lay thy sweet hands in mine and trust to me.

She laid her hands in his.

"And now, Mortie, darling," she said, "I want to tell you all about how I did the long twelfth at Auchtermuchtie in one under bogey."

Arnold Bennett

VERA'S FIRST CHRISTMAS
ADVENTURE

I

FIVE days before Christmas, Cheswardine came home to
his wife from a week's sojourn in London on business.
Vera, in her quality of the best-dressed woman in Bursley,
met him on the doorstep (or thereabouts) of their charming
but childless home, attired in a tea-gown that would have
ravished a far less impressionable male than her husband;
while he, in his quality of a prosaic and flourishing earthen-
ware manufacturer, pretended to take the tea-gown as a
matter of course, and gave her the sober, solid kiss of a man
who has been married six years and is getting used to it.

Still, the tea-gown had pleased him, and by certain secret
symptoms Vera knew that it had pleased him. She hoped
much from that tea-gown. She hoped that he had come home
in a more pacific temper than he had shown when he left her,
and that she would carry her point after all.

Now, naturally, when a husband in easy circumstances,
the possessor of a pretty and pampered wife, spends a week
in London and returns five days before Christmas certain
things are rightly and properly to be expected from him. It
would need an astounding courage, an amazing lack of a
sense of the amenity of conjugal existence in such a husband,
to enable him to disappoint such reasonable expectations.

And Cheswardine, though capable of pulling the curb very tight on the caprices of his wife, was a highly decent fellow. He had no intention to disappoint; he knew his duty.

So that during afternoon tea with the tea-gown in a cosy-corner of the great Chippendale drawing-room he began to unfasten a small wooden case which he had brought into the house in his own hand, opened it with considerable precaution, making a fine mess of packing-stuff on the carpet, and gradually drew to light a pair of vases of Venetian glass. He put them on the mantelpiece.

"There!" he said, proudly, and with a virtuous air.

They were obviously costly antique vases, exquisite in form, exquisite in the gradated tints of their pale blue and rose.

"Seventeenth century!" he said.

"They're very nice," Vera agreed, with a show of enthusiasm. "What are they for?"

"Your Christmas present," Cheswardine explained, and added, "my dear!"

"Oh, Stephen!" she murmured.

A kiss on these occasions is only just, and Cheswardine had one.

"Duveens told me they were quite unique," he said, modestly; "and I believe 'em."

You might imagine that a pair of Venetian vases of the seventeenth century, stated by Duveens to be unique, would have satisfied a woman who had a generous dress allowance and lacked absolutely nothing that was essential. But Vera was not satisfied. She was, on the contrary, profoundly disappointed. For the presence of those vases proved that she had not carried her point. They deprived her of hope. The unpleasantness before Cheswardine went to London had been more or less à propos of a Christmas present. Vera had seen in Bostock's vast emporium, in the neighbouring town of Hanbridge, a music-stool in the style known as *art nouveau*, which had enslaved her fancy. She had taken her husband to see it, and it had not enslaved her husband's fancy in the slightest degree. It was made in light woods, and the woods were curved and twisted as though they had recently spent seven years in a purgatory for sinful trees. Here and there in the design onyx-stones had been set in the wood. The seat itself was beautifully soft. What captured Vera was chiefly the fact that it did not open at the top, as most elaborate music-stools do, but at either side. You pressed a button (onyx) and the panel fell down displaying your music in little compartments ready to hand; and the eastern moiety of the music-stool was for piano pieces, and the western moiety for songs. In short, it was the last word of music-stools; nothing could possibly be newer.

But Cheswardine did not like it, and did not conceal his opinion. He argued that it would not "go" with the Chippendale furniture, and Vera said that all beautiful things "went" together, and Cheswardine admitted that they did, rather dryly. You see, they took the matter seriously because the house was their hobby; they were always changing its interior, which was more than they could have done for a child, even if they had had one; and Cheswardine's finer and soberer taste was always fighting against Vera's predilection for the novel and the bizarre. Apart from clothes, Vera had not much more than the taste of a mouse.

They did not quarrel in Bostock's. Indeed, they did not quarrel anywhere; but after Vera had suggested that he might at any rate humour her by giving her the music-stool for a Christmas present (she seemed to think this would somehow help it to "go" with the Chippendale), and Cheswardine had politely but firmly declined, there had been a certain coolness and quite six tears. Vera had caused it to be understood that even if Cheswardine was *not* interested in music, even if he did hate music and did call the Broadwood ebony grand ugly, that was no reason why she should be deprived of a pretty and original music-stool that would keep her music tidy and that would be *hers*. As for it not going with the Chippendale, that was simply an excuse . . . etc.

Hence, it is not surprising that the Venetian vases of the seventeenth century left Vera cold, and that the domestic prospects for Christmas were a little cold.

However, Vera, with wifely and submissive tact, made the best of things; and that evening she began to decorate the hall, dining-room, and drawing-room with holly and mistletoe. Before the pair retired to rest, the true Christmas feeling, slightly tinged with a tender melancholy, permeated the house, and the servants were growing excited in advance. The servants weren't going to have a dinner-party, with crackers and port and a table-centre unmatched in the Five Towns; the servants weren't going to invite their friends to an evening's jollity. The servants were merely going to work somewhat harder and have somewhat less sleep; but such is the magical effect of holly and mistletoe twined round picture-cords and hung under chandeliers that the excitement of the servants was entirely pleasurable.

And as Vera shut the bedroom door, she said, with a delightful, forgiving smile:

"I saw a lovely cigar-cabinet at Bostock's yesterday."

"Oh!" said Cheswardine, touched. He had no cigar-cabinet, and he wanted one, and Vera knew that he wanted one.

And Vera slept in the sweet consciousness of her thoughtful wifeliness.

The next morning at breakfast, Cheswardine demanded:

"Getting pretty hard up, aren't you, Maria?"

He called her Maria when he wished to be arch.

"Well," she said, "as a matter of fact, I am. What with the——"

And he gave her a five-pound note.

It happened so every year. He provided her with the money to buy him a Christmas present. But it is, I hope, unnecessary to say that the connection between her present to him and the money he furnished was never crudely mentioned.

She made an opportunity, before he left for the works, to praise the Venetian vases, and she insisted that he should wrap up well, because he was showing signs of one of his bad colds.

II

In the early afternoon she went to Bostock's emporium at Hanbridge to buy the cigar-cabinet and a few domestic trifles. Bostock's is a good shop. I do not say that it has the classic and serene dignity of Brunt's, over the way, where one orders one's dining-room suites and one's frocks for the January dances. But it is a good shop, and one of the chief glories of the Paris of the Five Towns. It has frontages in three streets, and it might be called the shop of the hundred windows. You can buy pretty nearly anything at Bostock's, from an *art nouveau* music-stool up to the highest cheese — for there is a provision department. (You can't get cheese at Brunt's.)

Vera made her uninteresting purchases first, in the basement, and then she went upstairs to the special Christmas department, which certainly was wonderful: a blaze and splendour of electric light; a glitter of gilded iridescent toys and knick-knacks; a smiling, excited, pushing multitude of faces, young and old; and the cashiers in their cages gathering in money as fast as they could lay their tired hands on it! A joyous, brilliant scene, calculated to bring soft tears of satisfaction to the board of directors that presided over Bostock's. It was a record Christmas for Bostock's. The electric cars were thundering over the frozen streets of all the Five Towns to bring customers to Bostock's. Children dreamt of Bostock's. Fathers went to scoff and remained to pay. Brunt's was not exactly alarmed, for nothing could alarm Brunt's; but there was just a sort of suspicion of something in the air at Brunt's that did not make for odious self-conceit. People seemed to become intoxicated when they went into Bostock's, to lose their heads in a frenzy of buying.

And there the *art nouveau* music-stool stood in the corner, where Vera had originally seen it! She approached it, not thinking of the terrible danger. The compartments for music lay invitingly open.

"Four pounds, nine and six, Mrs Cheswardine," said a shopwalker, who knew her.

She stopped to finger it.

Well, of course, everybody is acquainted with that peculiar ecstasy that undoubtedly does overtake you in good shops, sometimes, especially at Christmas. I prefer to call it ecstasy rather than intoxication, but I have heard it called even drunkenness. It is a magnificent and overwhelming experience, like a good wine. A blind instinct seizes your reason and throws her out of the window of your soul, and then assumes entire control of the volitional machinery. You listen to no arguments, you care for no consequences. You want a thing; you must have it; you do have it.

Vera was caught unawares by this magnificent and overwhelming experience, just as she stooped to finger the music-stool. A fig for the cigar-cabinet! A fig for her husband's objections! After all, she was a grown-up woman (twenty-nine or thirty), and entitled to a certain freedom. She was not and would not be a slave. It would look perfect in the drawing-room.

"I'll take it," she said.

"Yes, Mrs Cheswardine. A unique thing, quite unique. Penkethman!"

And Vera followed Penkethman to a cash desk and received half-a-guinea out of a five-pound note.

"I want it carefully packed," said Vera.

"Yes, ma'am. It will be delivered in the morning."

She was just beginning to realise that she had been under the sinister influence of the ecstasy, and that she had not bought the cigar-cabinet, and that she had practically no more money, and that Stephen's rule against credit was the strictest of all his rules, when she caught sight of Mr Charles Woodruff buying toys, doubtless for his nephews and nieces.

Mr Woodruff was the bachelor friend of the family. He had loved Vera before Stephen had loved her, and he was still attached to her. Stephen and he were chums of the most advanced kind. Why! Stephen and Vera thought nothing of bickering in front of Mr Woodruff, who rated them both and sided with neither.

"Hello!" said Woodruff, flushing, and moving his long, clumsy limbs when she touched him on the shoulder. "I'm just buying a few toys."

She helped him to buy toys, and then he asked her to go and have tea with him at the newly opened Sub Rosa Tea Rooms, in Machin Street. She agreed, and, in passing the music-stool, gave a small parcel which she was carrying to Penkethman, and told him he might as well put it in the music-stool. She was glad to have tea with Charlie Woodruff. It would distract her, prevent her from thinking. The ecstasy had almost died out, and she had a violent desire not to think.

III

A terrible blow fell upon her the next morning. Stephen had one of his bad colds, one of his worst. The mere cold she could have supported with fortitude, but he was forced to remain indoors, and his presence in the house she could not support with fortitude. The music-stool would be sure to arrive before lunch, and he would be there to see it arrive.

The ecstasy had fully expired now, and she had more leisure to think than she wanted. She could not imagine what mad instinct had compelled her to buy the music-stool. (Once out of the shop these instincts always are difficult to imagine.) She knew that Stephen would be angry. He might perhaps go to the length of returning the music-stool whence it came. For, though she was a pretty and pampered woman, Stephen had a way, in the last resort, of being master in his own house. And she could not even placate him with the gift of a cigar-cabinet. She could not buy a five-guinea cigar-cabinet with ten and six. She had no other money in the world. She never had money, yet money was always running through her fingers. Stephen treated her generously, gave her an ample allowance, but he would under no circumstances permit credit, nor would he pay her allowance in advance. She had nothing to expect till the New Year.

She attended to his cold, and telephoned to the works for a clerk to come up, and she refrained from telling Stephen that he must have been very careless while in London to catch a cold like that. Her self-denial in this respect surprised Stephen, but he put it down to the beneficent influence of Christmas and the Venetian vases.

Bostock's pair-horse van arrived before the garden gate earlier than her worst fears had anticipated, and Bostock's men were evidently in a tremendous hurry that morning. In quite an abnormally small number of seconds the wooden case containing the fragile music-stool was lying in the inner hall, waiting to be unpacked. Having signed the delivery-book, Vera stood staring at the accusatory package. Stephen was lounging over the dining-room fire, perhaps dozing. She would have the thing swiftly transported upstairs and hidden in an attic for a time.

But just then Stephen popped out of the dining-room. Stephen's masculine curiosity had been aroused by the advent of Bostock's van. He had observed the incoming of the package from the window, and he had ventured to the hall to inspect it. The event had roused him wonderfully from the heavy torpor which a cold induces. He wore a dressing-gown, the pockets of which bulged with handkerchiefs.

"You oughtn't to be out here, Stephen," said his wife.

"Nonsense!" he said. "Why, upon my soul, this steam heat is warmer than the dining-room fire."

Vera, silenced by the voice of truth, could not reply.

Stephen bent his great height to inspect the package. It was an appetising Christmas package; straw escaped from between its ribs, and it had an air of being filled with something at once large and delicate.

"Oh!" observed Stephen, humorously. "Ah! So this is it, is it? Ah! Oh! Very good!"

And he walked round it.

How on earth had he learnt that she had bought it? She had not mentioned the purchase to Mr Woodruff.

"Yes, Stephen," she said timidly. "That's it, and I hope——"

"It ought to hold a tidy few cigars, that ought," remarked Stephen complacently.

He took it for the cigar-cabinet!

She paused, struck. She had to make up her mind in an instant.

"Oh yes," she murmured.

"A thousand?"

"Yes, a thousand," she said.

"I thought so," murmured Stephen. "I mustn't kiss you, because I've got a cold," said he. "But, all the same, I'm awfully obliged, Vera. Suppose we have it opened now, eh? Then we could decide where it is to go, and I could put my cigars in it."

"Oh no," she protested. "Oh no, Stephen! That's not fair! It mustn't be opened before Christmas morning."

"But I gave you my vases yesterday."

"That's different," she said. "Christmas is Christmas."

"Oh, very well," he yielded. "That's all right, my dear."
Then he began to sniff.

"There's a deuced odd smell from it," he said.

"Perhaps it's the wood!" she faltered.

"I hope it isn't," he said. "I expect it's the straw. A deuced odd smell. We'll have the thing put in the side hall, next to the clock. It will be out of the way there. And I can come and gaze at it when I feel depressed. Eh, Maria?" He was undoubtedly charmed at the prospect of owning so large and precious a cigar-cabinet.

Considering that the parcel which she had given to Penkethman to put in the music-stool comprised half-a-pound of Bostock's very ripest Gorgonzola cheese, bought at the cook's special request, the smell which proceeded from the mysterious contents of the packing-case did not surprise Vera at all. But it disconcerted her none the less. And she wondered how she could get the cheese out.

For thirty hours the smell from the unopened packing-case waxed in vigour and strength. Stephen's cold grew worse and prevented him from appreciating its full beauty, but he savoured enough of it to induce him to compare it facetiously to the effluvium of a dead rat, and he said several times that Bostock's really ought to use better straw. He was frequently to be seen in the hall, gloating over his cigar-cabinet. Once he urged Vera to have it opened and so get rid of the straw, but she refused, and found the nerve to tell him that he was exaggerating the odour.

She was at a loss what to do. She could not get up in the middle of the night and unpack the package and hide its guilty secret. Indeed, to unpack the package would bring about her ruin instantly; for, the package unpacked, Stephen would naturally expect to see the cigar-cabinet. And so the hours crept on to Christmas and Vera's undoing. She gave herself a headache.

It was just thirty hours after the arrival of the package when Mr Woodruff dropped in for tea. Stephen was asleep in the dining-room, which apartment he particularly affected during his colds. Woodruff was shown into the drawing-room, where Vera was having her headache. Vera brightened. In fact, she suddenly grew very bright. And she gave Woodruff tea, and took some herself, and Woodruff passed an enjoyable twenty minutes.

The two Venetian vases were on the mantelpiece. Vera rose into ecstasies about them, and called upon Charlie Woodruff to rise too. He got up from his chair to examine the vases, which Vera had placed close together side by side at the corner of the mantelpiece nearest to him. Vera and Woodruff also stood close together side by side. And just as Woodruff was about to handle the vases, Vera knocked his arm; his arm collided with one vase; the vase collided with the next, and both fell to earth — to the hard, unfeeling, unyielding tiles of the hearth.

IV

They were smashed to atoms.

Vera screamed. She screamed twice, and ran out of the room.

"Stephen, Stephen!" she cried hysterically. "Charlie has broken my vases, both of them! It *is* too bad of him. He's really too clumsy!"

There was a terrific pother. Stephen wakened violently, and in a moment all three were staring ineffectually at the thousand crystal fragments on the hearth.

"But——" began Charlie Woodruff.

And that was all he did say.

He and Vera and Stephen had been friends since infancy, so she had the right not to conceal her feelings before him; Stephen had the same right. They both exercised it.

"But——" began Charlie again.

"Oh, never mind," Stephen stopped him curtly. "Accidents can't be helped."

"I shall get another pair," said Woodruff.

"No, you won't," replied Stephen. "You can't. There isn't another pair in the world. See?"

The two men simultaneously perceived that Vera was weeping. She was very pretty in tears, but that did not prevent the masculine world from feeling awkward and self-conscious. Charlie had notions about going out and burying himself.

"Come, Vera, come," her husband enjoined, blowing his nose with unnecessary energy, bad as his cold was.

"I — I liked those vases more than anything you've — you've ever given me," Vera blubbered, charmingly, patting her eyes.

Stephen glanced at Woodruff, as who should say: "Well, my boy, you uncorked those tears, I'll leave you to deal with 'em. You see, I'm an invalid in a dressing-gown. I leave you."

And went.

"No-but-look-here-I-say," Charlie Woodruff expostulated to Vera when he was alone with her — he often started an expostulation with that singular phrase. "I'm awfully sorry. I don't know how it happened. You must let me give you something else."

Vera shook her head.

"No," she said. "I wanted Stephen awfully to give me that music-stool that I told you about a fortnight ago. But he gave me the vases instead, and I liked them ever so much better."

"I shall give you the music-stool. If you wanted it a fortnight ago, you want it now. It won't make up for the vases, of course, but——"

"No, no," said Vera, positively.

"Why not?"

"I do not wish you to give me anything. It wouldn't be quite nice," Vera insisted.

"But I give you something every Christmas."

"Do you?" asked Vera, innocently.

"Yes, and you and Stephen give me something."

"Besides, Stephen doesn't quite like the music-stool."

"What's that got to do with it? You like it. I'm giving it to you, not to him. I shall go over to Bostock's tomorrow morning and get it."

"I forbid you to."

"I shall."

Woodruff departed.

Within five minutes the Cheswardine coachman was driving off in the dogcart to Hanbridge, with the packing-case in the back of the cart, and a note. He brought back the cigar-cabinet. Stephen had not stirred from the dining-room, afraid to encounter a tearful wife. Presently his wife came into the dining-room bearing the vast load of the cigar-cabinet in her delicate arms.

"I thought it might amuse you to fill it with your cigars — just to pass the time," she said.

Stephen's thought was: "Well, women take the cake." It was a thought that occurs frequently to husbands of Veras.

There was a ripe Gorgonzola at dinner. Stephen met it as one meets a person whom one fancies one has met somewhere but cannot remember where.

The next afternoon the music-stool came, for the second time, into the house. Charlie brought it in *his* dogcart. It was unpacked ostentatiously by the radiant Vera. What could Stephen say in depreciation of this gift from their oldest and best friend? As a fact, he could and did say a great deal. But he said it when he happened to be all alone in the drawing-room, and had observed the appalling way in which that music-stool did not "go" with the Chippendale.

"Look at the d—— thing!" he exclaimed to himself. "Look at it!"

However, the Christmas dinner-party was a brilliant success, and after it Vera sat on the *art nouveau* music-stool and twittered songs, and what with her being so attractive and birdlike, and what with the Christmas feeling in the air . . . well, Stephen resigned himself to the music-stool.

Saki

REGINALD'S CHRISTMAS REVEL

THEY say (said Reginald) that there's nothing sadder than victory except defeat. If you've ever stayed with dull people during what is alleged to be the festive season you can probably revise that saying. I shall never forget putting in a Christmas at the Babwolds'. Mrs Babwold is some relation of my father's — a sort of to-be-left till-called-for cousin — and that was considered sufficient reason for my having to accept her invitation at about the sixth time of asking; though why the sins of the father should be visited by the children — you won't find any notepaper in that drawer; that's where I keep old menus and first-night programmes.

Mrs Babwold wears a rather solemn personality, and has never been known to smile, even when saying disagreeable things to her friends or making out the Stores list. She takes her pleasures sadly. A state elephant at a Durbar gives one a very similar impression. Her husband gardens in all weathers. When a man goes out in the pouring rain to brush caterpillars off rose trees, I generally imagine his life indoors leaves something to be desired; anyway, it must be very unsettling for the caterpillars.

Of course there were other people there. There was a Major Somebody who had shot things in Lapland, or somewhere of that sort; I forget what they were, but it wasn't for want of reminding. We had them cold with every meal almost, and he was continually giving us details of what they measured from tip to tip, as though he thought we were going to make them warm under-things for the winter. I used to listen to him with a rapt attention that I thought rather suited me, and then one day I quite modestly gave the dimensions of an okapi I had shot in the Lincolnshire fens. The Major turned a beautiful Tyrian scarlet (I remember thinking at the time that I should like my bathroom hung in that colour), and I think that at that moment he almost found it in his heart to dislike me. Mrs Babwold put on a first-aid-to-the-injured expression, and asked him why he didn't publish a book of his sporting reminiscences; it would be *so* interesting. She didn't remember till afterwards that he had given her two fat volumes on the subject, with his portrait and autograph as a frontispeice and an appendix on the habits of the Arctic mussel.

It was in the evening that we cast aside the cares and distractions of the day and really lived. Cards were thought to be too frivolous and empty a way of passing the time, so most of them played what they called a book game. You went out into the hall — to get an inspiration, I suppose — then you came in again with a muffler tied round your neck and looked silly, and the others were supposed to guess that you were *Wee MacGreegor*. I held out against the inanity as long as I decently could, but at last, in a lapse of good-nature, I consented to masquerade as a book, only I warned them that it would take some time to carry out. They waited for the best part of forty minutes while I went and played wineglass skittles with the page-boy in the pantry; you play it with a champagne cork, you know, and the one who knocks down the most glasses without breaking them wins. I won, with four unbroken out of seven; I think William suffered from over-anxiousness. They were rather mad in the drawing-room at my not having come back, and they weren't a bit pacified when I told them afterwards that I was *At the end of the passage*.

"I never did like Kipling," was Mrs Babwold's comment, when the situation dawned upon her. "I couldn't see anything clever in *Earthworms out of Tuscany* — or is that by Darwin?"

Of course these games are very educational, but, personally, I prefer bridge.

On Christmas evening we were supposed to be specially festive in the Old English fashion. The hall was horribly draughty, but it seemed to be the proper place to revel in, and it was decorated with Japanese fans and Chinese lanterns, which gave it a very Old English effect. A young lady with a confidential voice favoured us with a long recitation about a little girl who died or did something equally hackneyed, and then the Major gave us a graphic account of a struggle he had with a wounded bear. I privately wished that the bears would win sometimes on these occasions; at least they wouldn't go vapouring about it afterwards. Before we had time to recover our spirits, we were indulged with some thought-reading by a young man whom one knew instinctively had a good mother and an indifferent tailor — the sort of young man who talks unflaggingly through the thickest soup, and smooths his hair dubiously as though he thought it might hit back. The thought-reading was rather a success; he announced that the hostess was thinking about poetry, and she admitted that her mind was dwelling on one of Austin's odes. Which was near enough. I fancy she had been really wondering whether a scrag-end of mutton and some cold plum-pudding would do for the kitchen dinner next day. As a crowning dissipation, they all sat down to play progressive halma, with milk-chocolate for prizes. I've been carefully brought up, and I don't like to play games of skill for milk-chocolate, so I invented a headache and retired from the scene. I had been preceded a few minutes earlier by Miss Langshan-Smith, a rather formidable lady, who always got up at some uncomfortable hour in the morning, and gave you the impression that she had been in communication with most of the European Governments before breakfast. There was a paper pinned on her door with a signed request that she might be called particularly early on the morrow. Such an opportunity does not come twice in a lifetime. I covered up everything except the signature with another notice, to the effect that before these words should meet the eye she would have ended a misspent life, was sorry for the trouble she was giving, and would like a military funeral. A few minutes later I violently exploded an air-filled paper bag on the landing, and gave a stage moan that could have been heard in the cellars. Then I pursued my original intention and went to bed. The noise those people made in forcing open the good lady's door was positively indecorous; she resisted gallantly, but I believe they searched her for bullets for about a quarter of an hour, as if she had been a historic battlefield.

I hate travelling on Boxing Day, but one must occasionally do things that one dislikes.

Stephen Leacock

A CHRISTMAS LETTER

IN ANSWER TO A YOUNG LADY WHO HAS SENT
AN INVITATION TO BE PRESENT AT A
CHILDREN'S PARTY

MADEMOISELLE, Allow me very gratefully but firmly
to refuse your kind invitation. You doubtless mean
well; but your ideas are unhappily mistaken.

Let us understand one another once and for all. I cannot at
my mature age participate in the sports of children with such
abandon as I could wish. I entertain, and have always entertained, the sincerest regard for such games at Hunt-the-
Slipper and Blind-Man's Buff. But I have now reached a
time of life, when, to have my eyes blindfolded and to have a
powerful boy of ten hit me in the back with a hobby-horse
and ask me to guess who hit me, provokes me to a fit of
retaliation which could only culminate in reckless
criminality. Nor can I cover my shoulders with a drawing-
room rug and crawl round on my hands and knees under the
pretence that I am a bear without a sense of personal
insufficiency, which is painful to me.

Neither can I look on with a complacent eye at the sad
spectacle of your young clerical friend, the Reverend Mr
Uttermost Farthing, abandoning himself to such gambols
and appearing in the rôle of life and soul of the evening.
Such a degradation of his holy calling grieves me, and I
cannot but suspect him of ulterior motives.

You inform me that your maiden aunt intends to help you entertain the party. I have not, as you know, the honour of your aunt's acquaintance, yet I think I may with reason surmise that she will organise games — guessing games — in which she will ask me to name a river in Asia beginning with a Z; on my failure to do so she will put a hot plate down my neck as a forfeit, and the children will clap their hands. These games, my dear young friend, involve the use of a more adaptable intellect than mine, and I cannot consent to be a party to them.

May I say in conclusion that I do not consider a five-cent pen-wiper from the top branch of a Xmas tree any adequate compensation for the kind of evening you propose.

I have the honour

To subscribe myself,

Your obedient servant.

Samuel Pepys

FROM THE DIARIES

CHRISTMAS DAY, 1660. In the morning very much pleased to see my house once more clear of workmen and to be clean; and endeed it is so far better then it was, that I do not repent of my trouble that I have been at.

In the morning to church; where Mr Mills made a very good sermon. After that home to dinner, where my wife and I and my brother Tom (who this morning came to see my wife's new mantle put on, which doth please me very well) — to a good shoulder of Mutton and a Chicken. After dinner to church again, my wife and I, where we have a dull sermon of a stranger which made me sleep; and so home; and I, before and after supper, to my Lute and Fullers *History*, at which I stayed all alone in my Chamber till 12 at night; and so to bed.

CHRISTMAS DAY, 1661. In the morning to church; where at the door of our pew I was fain to stay, because that the Sexton had not opened the door. A good sermon of Mr Mills. Dined at home all alone. And taking occasion, from some fault in the meat, to complain of my maid's Sluttery, my wife and I fell out, and I up to my Chamber in a discontent. After dinner my wife comes up to me and all friends again; and she and I to walk upon the Leads; and there Sir W. Pen called us and we went to his house and supped with him. But before supper, Captain Cock came to us half-drunck and begun to talk; but Sir W. Pen, knowing his humour and that there was

no end of his talking, drinks four great glasses of wine to him
one after another, healths to the King &c., and by that means
made him drunk, and so he went away; and so we sat down to
supper and were merry; and so after supper home and to bed.

CHRISTMAS DAY, 1662. Up pretty early, leaving my wife
not well in bed. And with my boy walked, it being a most
brave cold and dry frosty morning, and had a pleasant walk
to Whitehall; where I entended to have received the
Comunion with the family, but I came a little too late. So I
walked up into the house and spent my time looking over
pictures, perticularly the ships in King H the 8ths voyage to
Bullen — marking the great difference between their build
then and now. By and by down to the Chappell again, where
Bishop Morly preached upon the Song of the Angels —
"Glory to God on high — on earth peace, and good will
towards men". Methought he made but a poor sermon, but
long and reprehending the mistaken jollity of the Court for
the true joy that shall and ought to be on these days.
Perticularized concerning their excess in playes and
gameing, saying that he whose office is to keep the
Gamesters in order and within bounds serves but for a second
rather in a Duell, meaning the Groome porter. Upon which,
it was worth observing how far they are come from taking
the Reprehensions of a Bishop seriously, that they all laugh
in the chapel when he reflected on their ill actions and
courses.

He did much press us to joy in these public days of joy and
to Hospitality. But one that stood by whispered in my eare
that the Bishop himself doth not spend one groate to the poor
himself.

The sermon done, a good Anthemne fallowed, with vialls;
and then the King came down to receive the Sacrament, but I
stayed not; but calling my boy from my Lord's lodging and
giving Sarah some good advice, by my Lord's order, to be
Sober and look after the house, I walked home again with

great pleasure; and there dined by my wife's bedside with great content, having a mess of brave plum-porridge and a roasted Pullett for dinner; and I sent for a mince-pie abroad, my wife not being well to make any herself yet. After dinner sat talking a good while with her, her [pain] being become less, and then to see Sir W. Penn a little; and so to my office, practising arithmetique alone and making an end of last night's book, with great content, till 11 at night; and so home to supper and to bed.

CHRISTMAS DAY, 1663. Lay long, talking pleasantly with my wife; but among other things, she begin, I know not whether by design or chance, to enquire what she should do if I should by an accident die; to which I did give her some slight answer, but shall make good use of it to bring myself to some settlement for her sake, by making a Will as soon as I can.

Up, and to church, where Mr Mills made an ordinary sermon; and so home and dined with great pleasure with my wife; and all the afternoon, first looking out at window and seeing the boys playing at many several sports in our back-yard by Sir W. Pens, which minded me of my own former times; and then I begin to read to my wife upon the globes, with great pleasure and to good purpose, for it will be pleasant to her and to me to have her understand those things.

In the evening to the office, where I stayed late reading Rushworth, which is a most excellent collection of the beginning of the late quarrels in this kingdom. And so home to supper and to bed with good content of mind.

CHRISTMAS DAY, 1664. Up (my wife's eye being ill still of the blow I did in a passion give her on Monday last) to church alone — where Mr Mills, a good sermon. To dinner at home, where very pleasant with my wife and family. After dinner, I to Sir W. Batten's and there received so much good usage (as I have of late done) from him and my Lady, obliging me and my wife, according to promise, to come and dine with them tomorrow with our neighbours, that I was in pain all the day, and night too after, to know how to order the business of my wife's not going — and by discourse receive fresh instances of Sir J. Minnes's folly in complaining to Sir G. Carteret of Sir W. Batten and me for some family offences; such as my having of a stopcock to keep the water from them — which vexes me, but it would more, but that Sir G. Carteret knows him very well. Thence to the French church; but coming too late, I returned and to Mr Rawlinson's church, where I heard a good semon of one that I remember was at Pauls with me, his name Maggett. And very great store of fine women there is in this church, more then I know anywhere else about us.

So home and to my chamber, looking over and setting in order my papers and books; and so to supper, and then to prayers and to bed.

CHRISTMAS DAY, 1665. To church in the morning, and there saw a wedding in the church, which I have not seen many a day, and the young people so merry one with another; and strange, to see what delight we married people have to see these poor fools decoyed into our condition, every man and wife gazing and smiling at them. Here I saw again my beauty Lethulier. Thence to my Lord Brouncker by invitation, and dined there — and so home to my lodgings to settle myself to look over and settle my papers, both of my accounts private and those of Tanger, which I have let go so long that it were impossible for any soul, had I died, to understand them or ever come to any good end in them. I hope God will never suffer me to come to that disorder again.

CHRISTMAS DAY, 1666. Lay pretty long in bed. And then rise, leaving my wife desirous to sleep, having sat up till 4 this morning seeing her maids make mince-pies. I to church, where our parson Mills made a good sermon. Then home, and dined well on some good ribbs of beef roasted and mince pies; only my wife, brother, and Barker, and plenty of good wine of my own; and my heart full of true joy and thanks to God Almighty for the goodness of my condition at this day. After dinner I begun to teach my wife and Barker my song, *It is decreed* — which pleases me mightily, as now I have Mr Hinxton's bass. Then out, and walked alone on foot to Temple, it being a fine frost, thinking to have seen a play all alone; but there missing of any Bills, concluded there was none; and so back home, and there with my brother, reducing the names of all my books to an Alphabet, which kept us till 7 or 8 at night; and then to supper, W. Hewer with us, and pretty merry; and then to my chamber to enter this day's journal only, and then to bed — my head a little thoughtful how [to] behave myself in the business of the victualling, which I think will be prudence to offer my service in doing something in passing the purser's accounts — thereby to serve the King — get honour to myself, and confirm me in my place in the victualling, which at present hath not work enough to deserve my wages.

CHRISTMAS EVE, 1667. Up, and all the morning at the office; and at noon with my clerks to dinner and then to the office again, busy at the office till 6 at night; and then by coach to St. James's, it being now about 6 at night, my design being to see the Ceremonys, this night being the Eve of Christmas, at the Queen's Chapel. But it being not begun, I to Westminster hall and there stayed and walked; and then to the Swan and there drank and talked, and did besar a little Frank; and so to White-hall and sent my coach round, and I through the park to chapel, where I got in up almost to the rail and with a great deal of patience, stayed from 9 at night to 2 in the morning in a very great Crowd; and there expected, but found nothing extraordinary, there being

nothing but a high Masse. The Queen was there and some
ladies. But Lord, what an odde thing it was for me to be in a
crowd of people, here a footman, there a beggar, here a fine
lady, there a zealous poor papist, and here a Protestant, two
or three together, come to see the show. I was afeared of my
pocket being picked very much. But here I did make myself
to do la cosa by mere imagination, mirando a jolie mosa and
with my eyes open, which I never did before — and God
forgive me for it, it being in the chapel. Their music very
good endeed, but their service I confess too frivolous, that
there can be no zeal go along with it; and I do find by them
themselfs, that they do run over their beads with one hand,
and point and play and talk and make signs with the other, in
the midst of their Messe. But all things very rich and
beautiful. And I see the papists had the wit, most of them, to
bring cushions to kneel on; which I wanted, and was
mightily troubled to kneel. All being done, and I sorry for
my coming, missing of what I expected; which was to have
had a child borne and dressed there and a great deal of do, but
we broke up and nothing like it done; and there I left people
receiving the sacrament, and the Queen gone, and ladies;
only my [Lady] Castlemayne, who looks prettily in her
night-clothes. And so took my coach, which waited, and
away through Covent-garden to set down two gentlemen
and a lady, who came thither to see also and did make mighty
mirth in their talk of the folly of this religion; and so I
stopped, having set them down, and drank some burnt wine
at the Rose tavern door, while the constables came and two
or three Bell-men went by, it being a fine light [25th]
moonshine morning; and so home round the City and
stopped and dropped money at five or six places, which I was
the willinger to do, it being Christmas-day; and so home and
there find wife in bed, and Jane and the maids making pyes,
and so I to bed and slept well; and rose about 9, and to church
and there heard a dull sermon of Mr Mills, but a great many
fine people at church, and so home; wife and girl and I alone

at dinner, a good Christmas dinner; and all the afternoon at home, my wife reading to me the history of the Drummer, of Mr Monpesson, which is a strange story of spirits, and worth reading indeed. In the evening comes Mr Pelling, and he sat and supped with us; and very good company, he reciting to us many copies of good verses of Dr Wilde, who writ *Iter Boreale*; and so to bed — my boy being gone with W. Hewer and Mr Hater to Mr Gibsons in the country to dinner, and lie there all night.

CHRISTMAS DAY, 1668. Up, and continued on my waist-coat, the first day this winter. And I to church, where Alderman Backewell coming in late, I beckoned to his lady to come up to us; who did, with another lady; and after sermon I led her down through the church to her husband and coach — a noble, fine woman, and a good one — and one my wife shall be acquainted with. So home and to dinner alone with my wife, who, poor wretch, sat undressed all day till 10 at night, altering and lacing of a black petticoat — while I by her, making the boy read to me the life of Julius Caesar and Des Cartes book of music — the latter of which I understand not, nor think he did well that writ it, though a most learned man. Then after supper made the boy play upon his lute, which I have not done twice before sence he came to me; and so, my mind in mighty content, we to bed.

Joseph Addison

SIR ROGER ON CHRISTMAS

H E afterwards fell into an Account of the Diversions which had passed in his House during the Holydays, for Sir ROGER, after the laudable Custom of his Ancestors, always keeps open-House at *Christmas*. I learned from him, that he had killed eight fat Hogs for this Season, that he had dealt about his Chines very liberally amongst his Neighbours, and that in particular he had sent a string of Hogs-puddings with a pack of Cards to every poor Family in the Parish. I have often thought, says Sir ROGER, it happens very well that *Christmas* should fall out in the middle of Winter. It is the most dead, uncomfortable time of the Year, when the poor People would suffer very much from their Poverty and Cold, if they had not good Cheer, warm Fires, and *Christmas* Gambols to support them. I love to rejoyce their poor Hearts at this Season, and to see the whole Village merry in my great Hall. I allow a double quantity of Malt to my small Beer, and set it a running for twelve Days to every one that calls for it. I have always a Piece of cold Beef and a Mince-Pye upon the Table, and am wonderfully pleased to see my Tenants pass away a whole Evening in playing their innocent Tricks, and smutting one another. Our Friend *Will. Wimble* is as merry as any of them, and shews a thousand Roguish Tricks upon these Occasions.

I was very much delighted with the Reflection of my old Friend, which carried so much Goodness in it. He then launched out into the Praise of the late Act of Parliament for securing the Church of *England*, and told me, with great Satisfaction, that he believed it already began to take Effect; for that a rigid Dissenter, who chanced to Dine at his House on *Christmas* Day, had been observed to Eat very plentifully of his Plumb-porridge.

Thomas Babington Macaulay

FROM THE
HISTORY OF ENGLAND

PERHAPS no single circumstance more strongly illus-
trates the temper of the precisians than their conduct
respecting Christmas day. Christmas had been, from time
immemorial, the season of joy and domestic affection, the
season when families assembled, when children came home
from school, when quarrels were made up, when carols were
heard in every street, when every house was decorated with
evergreens, and every table was loaded with good cheer. At
that season all hearts not utterly destitute of kindness were
enlarged and softened. At that season the poor were
admitted to partake largely of the overflowings of the
wealth of the rich, whose bounty was peculiarly acceptable
on account of the shortness of the days and of the severity of
the weather. At that season the interval between landlord
and tenant, master and servant, was less marked than
through the rest of the year. Where there is much enjoyment
there will be some excess: yet, on the whole, the spirit in
which the holiday was kept was not unworthy of a Christian
festival. The Long Parliament gave orders, in 1644, that the
twenty-fifth of December should be strictly observed as a
fast, and that all men should pass it in humbly bemoaning the
great national sin which they and their fathers had so often
committed on that day by romping under the mistletoe,
eating boar's head and drinking ale flavoured with roasted

apples. No public act of that time seems to have irritated the common people more. On the next anniversary of the festival formidable riots broke out in many places. The constables were resisted, the magistrates insulted, the houses of noted zealots attacked, and the proscribed service of the day openly read in the churches.

Piers Compton

ALL QUIET FOR CHRISTMAS

IT was going to be a bitter Christmas. Weather experts predicted a spell of hard frosty weather. . . .

It was the first Christmas of the Great War, 1914. Half the nations of Europe were engaged in a life-or-death struggle. Thousands of men faced each other in trenches spread like an elongated maze across Belgium and France.

Force, not wisdom, was the order of the day. The pleas for a Christmas truce made by Pope Benedict XV had been disregarded by both sides. . . .

But although the leaders in London and Berlin could remain impervious to the Christmas appeal, there were signs that the men in the firing zone were ready to respond.

On Christmas eve a party from the Medical Corps wandered into the ruined town of Ypres. The cathedral was shattered but the organ had not been touched, and one of the party settled himself at the keyboard.

How far the notes penetrated we shall never know, but with devastation all about them, and with guns booming in the near distance, he played some verses of *Adeste Fideles*.

It was, as predicted, a day of hard frost. With the coming of darkness, when things quietened down, fires were lighted in the trenches where strange rumours were being circulated. The rumours had no official sanction. No one knew exactly how or where they came into being. There was no definite arrangement, and conditions differed all down the line. But it soon became generally known that German and British had promised to cease fire throughout Christmas Day.

In some sectors the British could see coloured lights and candles burning along the top of the German trenches.

Here and there a Christmas tree was set up on the parapet. And something of the holiness, the magic of Christmas, entered into the suddenly quiet world of war.

Rifles were kept near at hand. . . . But no one fired. Instead groups of British and Germans clambered out of their trenches, worked round the barbed wire, and met together in the snowy desolation of No Man's Land. The cry of no shooting became general. It seems that the British, at the start, were more suspicious than the Germans, for the latter were heard calling: "Come out, you British!". At one point they hoisted a placard wishing their enemies "A happy Christmas". At another, in front of the trenches held by the Scots Guards, they revealed the efficiency of their intelligence service by displaying a board with the message: "A merry Christmas, Scottie Guardie".

A line was drawn half-way between the trenches, and here the fighting men met, regarding each other curiously at first, the officers saluting each other and shaking hands, the Germans, very polite and clicking their heels with a bow. Conversation was sometimes difficult, but an interpreter could always be found before long.

Both sides agreed not to take advantage of the lull by improving or repairing their barbed wire defences. It was also agreed that if a shot was accidentally fired it would not be regarded as an act of war, and that an apology would be accepted.

They exchanged the chocolate, cigars and cigarettes received in their Christmas parcels. Cap badges and buttons were given as souvenirs. One German produced a bottle of wine and asked the British to drink their king's health. . . .

Those Germans who knew London indulged in reminiscences of Marble Arch and "Peecadeely". A British battalion played a Saxon team at football and the Saxons won 3-2.

The only serious business of the day was the burying of the dead. Both sides dug graves for those who had fallen in front of the trenches, and the British supplied some wooden crosses. One party of Germans came forward bareheaded, and bearing the body of a British officer who had fallen behind their lines. Another gathering took place in a turnip field where some Germans, to mouth-organ accompaniment, did a queer sort of hopping dance that caused amusement.

There were sectors where the British were invited to visit the German trenches. Those who did so stayed for some time, and reported afterwards that they had been very well entertained. And so the day passed. The early darkness of a cold frosty night came on, and the strangely mixed company gathered for a sing-song. They entertained each other by singing in turn, and here the Germans were, of course, more competent and knowledgeable than the British, whose repertoire was usually restricted to popular songs or snatches of a carol.

The German contributions varied from "Tipperary" and "Home Sweet Home" to a fine Saxon rendering of "God Save the King". An excellent baritone overcame the narrow sense of nationality that divided his audience with Schuman's "Two Grenadiers". A cornet player (he must be professional, thought the British) warmed their hearts with sentimental airs.

The two sides applauded each other. Sometimes a flare went up, and the now superfluous light was greeted with new bursts of cheering and waving of caps.

But all too soon it was midnight. The men said goodbye to each other with more handshakes and the clicking of heels; and the next flare illumined a deserted No Man's Land and the wraiths of barbed wire overlooking the imminence of death. . . .

Percy Mackaye

CHRISTMAS, 1915

NOW is the midnight of the nations: dark
   Even as death, beside her blood-dark seas,
Earth, like a mother in birth agonies,
Screams in her travail, and the planets hark
Her million-throated terror. Naked, stark,
Her torso writhes enormous, and her knees
Shudder against the shadowed Pleiades,
Wrenching the night's imponderable arc.

Christ! What shall be delivered to the morn
Out of these pangs, if ever indeed another
Morn shall succeed this night, or this vast mother
Survive to know the blood-sprent offspring, torn
From her racked flesh?—What splendor from the smother?
What new-wing'd world, or mangled god still-born?

T. M. Kettle

TO MY DAUGHTER BETTY

IN wiser days, my darling rosebud, blown
   To beauty proud as was your Mother's prime.
In that desired, delayed, incredible time,
You'll ask why I abandoned you, my own,
And the dear heart that was your baby throne,
To dice with death. And oh! they'll give you rhyme
And reason: some will call the thing sublime,
And some decry it in a knowing tone.
So here, while the mad guns curse overhead,
And tired men sigh with mud for couch and floor,
Know that we fools, now with the foolish dead,
Died not for flag, nor King, nor Emperor,
But for a dream, born in a herdsman's shed,
And for the secret Scripture of the poor.

Thomas Hardy

CHRISTMAS, 1924

"PEACE upon earth!" was said. We sing it,
    And pay a million priests to bring it.
After two thousand years of mass
We've got as far as poison-gas.

Nathaniel Hawthorne

THE CHRISTMAS BANQUET

"**I** HAVE here attempted," said Roderick, unfolding a few sheets of manuscript, as he sat with Rosina and the sculptor in the summer house, — "I have attempted to seize hold of a personage who glides past me, occasionally, in my walk through life. My former sad experience, as you know, has gifted me with some degree of insight into the gloomy mysteries of the human heart, through which I have wandered like one astray in a dark cavern, with his torch fast flickering to extinction. But this man, this class of men, is a hopeless puzzle."

"Well, but propound him," said the sculptor. "Let us have an idea of him, to begin with."

"Why, indeed," replied Roderick, "he is such a being as I could conceive you to carve out of marble, and some yet unrealised perfection of human science to endow with an exquisite mockery of intellect; but still there lacks the last inestimable touch of a divine Creator. He looks like a man; and, perchance, like a better specimen of man than you ordinarily meet. You might esteem him wise; he is capable of cultivation and refinement, and has at least an external conscience; but the demands that spirit makes upon spirit are precisely those to which he cannot respond. When at last you come close to him you find him chill and unsubstantial, — a mere vapour."

"I believe," said Rosina, "I have a glimmering idea of what you mean."

"Then be thankful," answered her husband, smiling; "but do not anticipate any further illumination from what I am about to read. I have here imagined such a man to be — what, probably, he never is — conscious of the deficiency in his spiritual organisation. Methinks the result would be a sense of cold unreality wherewith he would go shivering through the world, longing to exchange his load of ice for any burden of real grief that fate could fling upon a human being."

Contenting himself with this preface, Roderick began to read.

In a certain old gentleman's last will and testament there appeared a bequest, which, as his final thought and deed, was singularly in keeping with a long life of melancholy eccentricity. He devised a considerable sum for establishing a fund, the interest of which was to be expended annually forever, in preparing a Christmas Banquet for ten of the most miserable persons that could be found. It seemed not to be the testator's purpose to make these half a score of sad hearts merry, but to provide that the stern or fierce expression of human discontent should not be drowned, even for that one holy and joyful day, amid the acclamations of festal gratitude which all Christendom sends up. And he desired, likewise, to perpetuate his own remonstrance against the earthly course of Providence, and his sad and sour dissent from those systems of religion or philosophy which either find sunshine in the world or draw it down from heaven.

The task of inviting the guests, or of selecting among such as might advance their claims to partake of this dismal hospitality, was confided to the two trustees or stewards of the fund. These gentlemen, like their deceased friend, were sombre humorists, who made it their principal occupation to number the sable threads in the web of human life, and drop all the golden ones out of the reckoning. They performed their present office with integrity and judgement. The aspect of the assembled company, on the day of the first festival, might not, it is true, have satisfied every beholder that these were especially the individuals, chosen forth from all the world, whose griefs were worthy to stand as indicators of the mass of human suffering. Yet, after due consideration, it could not be disputed that here was a variety of hopeless discomfort, which, if it sometimes arose from causes apparently inadequate, was thereby only the shrewder imputation against the nature and mechanism of life.

The arrangements and decorations of the banquet were probably intended to signify that death in life which had been the testator's definition of existence. The hall, illuminated by torches, was hung round with curtains of deep and dusky purple, and adorned with branches of cypress and wreaths of artificial flowers, imitative of such as used to be strewn over the dead. A sprig of parsley was laid by every plate. The main reservoir of wine was a sepulchral urn of silver, whence the liquor was distributed around the table in small vases, accurately copied from those that held the tears of ancient mourners. Neither had the stewards — if it were their taste that arranged these details — forgotten the fantasy of the old Egyptians, who seated a skeleton at every festive board, and mocked their own merriment with the imperturbable grin of a death's-head. Such a fearful guest, shrouded in a black mantle, sat now at the head of the table. It was whispered, I know not with what truth, that the testator himself had once walked the visible world with the machinery of that same skeleton, and that it was one of the stipulations of his will, that he should thus be permitted to sit, from year to year, at the banquet which he had instituted. If so, it was perhaps covertly implied that he had cherished no hopes of bliss beyond the grave to compensate for the evils which he felt or imagined here. And if, in their bewildered conjectures as to the purpose of earthly existence, the banqueters should throw aside the veil, and cast an inquiring glance at this figure of death, as seeking thence the solution otherwise unattainable, the only reply would be a stare of the vacant eye-caverns and a grin of skeleton jaws. Such was the response that the dead man had fancied himself to receive when he asked of Death to solve the riddle of his life; and it was his desire to repeat it when the guests of his dismal hospitality should find themselves perplexed with the same question.

"What means that wreath?" asked several of the company, while viewing the decorations of the table.

They alluded to a wreath of cypress, which was held on high by a skeleton arm, protruding from within the black mantle.

"It is a crown," said one of the stewards, "not for the worthiest, but for the wofulest, when he shall prove his claim to it."

The guest earliest bidden to the festival was a man of soft and gentle character, who had not energy to struggle against the heavy despondency to which his temperament rendered him liable; and therefore with nothing outwardly to excuse him from happiness, he had spent a life of quiet misery that made his blood torpid, and weighed upon his breath, and sat like a ponderous night-fiend upon every throb of his unresisting heart. His wretchedness seemed as deep as his original nature, if not identical with it. It was the misfortune of a second guest to cherish within his bosom a diseased heart, which had become so wretchedly sore that the continual and unavoidable rubs of the world, the blow of an enemy, the careless jostle of a stranger, and even the faithful and loving touch of a friend, alike made ulcers in it. As is the habit of people thus afflicted, he found his chief employment in exhibiting these miserable sores to any who would give themselves the pain of viewing them. A third guest was a hypochondriac, whose imagination wrought necromancy in his outward and inward world, and caused him to see monstrous faces in the household fire, and dragons in the clouds of sunset, and fiends in the guise of beautiful women, and something ugly or wicked beneath all the pleasant surfaces of nature. His neighbour at table was one who, in his early youth, had trusted mankind too much, and hoped too highly in their behalf, and, in meeting with many disappointments, had become desperately soured. For several years back this misanthrope had employed himself in accumulating motives for hating and despising his race, — such as murder, lust, treachery, ingratitude, faithlessness of trusted friends, instinctive vices of children, impurity of women, hidden guilt in men of saint-like aspect, — and, in short, all manner of black realities that sought to decorate themselves with outward grace or glory. But at every atrocious fact that was added to his catalogue, at every increase of the sad knowledge which he spent his life to collect, the native impulses of the poor man's loving and confiding heart made him groan with anguish. Next, with his heavy brow bent downward, there stole into the hall a man naturally earnest and impassioned, who, from his immemorial infancy, had felt the consciousness of a high message to the world; but, essaying to deliver it, had found either no voice or form of speech, or else no ears to listen. Therefore his whole life was a bitter questioning of himself: "Why have not men acknowledged my mission? Am I not a self-deluding fool? What business have I on earth? Where is my grave?" Throughout the festival, he quaffed frequent draughts from the sepulchral urn of wine, hoping thus to quench the celestial fire that tortured his own breast and could not benefit his race.

Then there entered, having flung away a ticket for a ball, a gay gallant of yesterday, who had found four or five wrinkles in his brow, and more gray hairs than he could well number on his head. Endowed with sense and feeling, he had nevertheless spent his youth in folly, but had reached at last that dreary point in life where Folly quits us of her own accord, leaving us to make friends with Wisdom if we can. Thus, cold and desolate, he had come to seek Wisdom at the banquet, and wondered if the skeleton were she. To eke out the company, the stewards had invited a distressed poet from his home in the almshouse, and a melancholy idiot from the street-corner. The latter had just the glimmering of sense that was sufficient to make him conscious of a vacancy, which the poor fellow, all his life long, had mistily sought to fill up with intelligence, wandering up and down the streets, and groaning miserably because his attempts were ineffectual. The only lady in the hall was one who had fallen short of absolute and perfect beauty, merely by the trifling defect of a slight cast in her left eye. But this blemish, minute as it was, so shocked the pure ideal of her soul, rather than her vanity, that she passed her life in solitude, and veiled her countenance even from her own gaze. So the skeleton sat shrouded at one end of the table, and this poor lady at the other.

One other guest remains to be described. He was a young man of smooth brow, fair cheek, and fashionable mien. So far as his exterior developed him, he might much more suitably have found a place at some merry Christmas table, than have been numbered among the blighted, fate-stricken, fancy-tortured set of ill-starred banqueters. Murmurs arose among the guests as they noted the glance of general scrutiny which the intruder threw over his companions. What had he to do among them? Why did not the skeleton of the dead founder of the feast unbend its rattling joints, arise, and motion the unwelcome stranger from the board?

"Shameful!" said the morbid man, while a new ulcer broke out in his heart. "He comes to mock us! — we shall be the jest of his tavern friends! — he will make a farce of our miseries, and bring it out upon the stage!"

"Oh, never mind him!" said the hypochondriac, smiling sourly. "He shall feast from yonder tureen of viper-soup; and if there is a fricassee of scorpions on the table, pray let him have his share of it. For the dessert, he shall taste the apples of Sodom. Then, if he like our Christmas fare, let him return again next year!"

"Trouble him not," murmured the melancholy man, with gentleness. "What matters it whether the consciousness of misery come a few years sooner or later? If this youth deem himself happy now, yet let him sit with us for the sake of the wretchedness to come."

The poor idiot approached the young man with that mournful aspect of vacant inquiry which his face continually wore, and which caused people to say that he was always in search of his missing wits. After no little examination he touched the stranger's hand, but immediately drew back his own, shaking his head and shivering.

"Cold, cold, cold!" muttered the idiot.

The young man shivered too, and smiled.

"Gentlemen, and you, madam, said one of the stewards of the festival, "do not conceive so ill either of our caution or judgement, as to imagine that we have admitted this young stranger — Gervayse Hastings by name — without a full investigation and thoughtful balance of his claims. Trust me, not a guest at the table is better entitled to his seat."

The steward's guaranty was perforce satisfactory. The company, therefore, took their places, and addressed themselves to the serious business of the feast, but were soon disturbed by the hypochondriac, who thrust back his chair, complaining that a dish of stewed toads and vipers was set before him, and that there was green ditchwater in his cup of wine. This mistake being amended, he quietly resumed his seat. The wine, as it flowed freely from the sepulchral urn, seemed to come imbued with all gloomy inspirations; so that its influence was not to cheer, but either to sink the revellers into a deeper melancholy, or elevate their spirits to an enthusiasm of wretchedness. The conversation was various. They told sad stories about people who might have been worthy guests at such a festival as the present. They talked of grisly incidents in human history; of strange crimes, which, if truly considered, were but convulsions of agony; of some lives that had been altogether wretched, and of others which, wearing a general semblance of happiness, had yet been deformed, sooner or later, by misfortune, as by the intrusion of a grim face at a banquet; of deathbed scenes, and what dark intimations might be gathered from the words of dying men; of suicide, and whether the more eligible mode were by halter, knife, poison, drowning, gradual starvation, or the fumes of charcoal. The majority of the guests, as is the custom with people thoroughly and profoundly sick at heart, were anxious to make their own woes the theme of discussion, and prove themselves most excellent in anguish. The misanthropist went deep into the philosophy of evil, and wandered about in the darkness, with now and then a gleam of discoloured light hovering on ghastly shapes and horrid scenery. Many a miserable thought, such as men have stumbled upon from age to age, did he now rake up again, and gloat over it as an inestimable gem, a diamond, a treasure far preferable to those bright, spiritual revelations of a better world, which are like precious stones from heaven's pavement. And then, amid his lore of wretchedness he hid his face and wept.

It was a festival at which the woful man of Uz might suitably have been a guest, together with all, in each succeeding age, who have tasted deepest of the bitterness of life. And be it said, too, that every son or daughter of woman, however favoured with happy fortune, might, at one sad moment or another, have claimed the privilege of a stricken heart, to sit down at this table. But throughout the feast it was remarked that the young stranger, Gervayse Hastings, was unsuccessful in his attempts to catch its pervading spirit. At any deep, strong thought that found utterance, and which was torn out, as it were, from the saddest recesses of human consciousness, he looked mystified and bewildered; even more than the poor idiot, who seemed to grasp at such things with his earnest heart, and thus occasionally to comprehend them. The young man's conversation was of a colder and lighter kind, often brilliant, but lacking the powerful characteristics of a nature that had been developed by suffering.

"Sir," said the misanthropist, bluntly, in reply to some observation by Gervayse Hastings, "pray do not address me again. We have no right to talk together. Our minds have nothing in common. By what claim you appear at this banquet I cannot guess; but methinks, to a man who could say what you have just now said, my companions and myself must seem no more than shadows flickering on the wall. And precisely such a shadow are you to us."

The young man smiled and bowed, but, drawing himself back in his chair, he buttoned his coat over his breast, as if the banqueting-hall were growing chill. Again the idiot fixed his melancholy stare upon the youth, and murmured, "Cold! cold! cold!"

The banquet drew to its conclusion, and the guests departed. Scarcely had they stepped across the threshold of the hall, when the scene that had there passed seemed like the vision of a sick fancy, or an exhalation from a stagnant heart. Now and then, however, during the year that ensued, these melancholy people caught glimpses of one another, transient, indeed, but enough to prove that they walked the earth with the ordinary allotment of reality. Sometimes a pair of them came face to face, while stealing through the evening twilight, enveloped in their sable cloaks. Sometimes they casually met in churchyards. Once, also, it happened that two of the dismal banqueters mutually started at recognising each other in the noonday sunshine of a crowded street, stalking there like ghosts astray. Doubtless they wondered why the skeleton did not come abroad at noonday too.

But whenever the necessity of their affairs compelled these Christmas guests into the bustling world, they were sure to encounter the young man who had so unaccountably been admitted to the festival. They saw him among the gay and fortunate; they caught the sunny sparkle of his eye; they heard the light and careless tones of his voice, and muttered to themselves with such indignation as only the aristocracy of wretchedness could kindle, "The traitor! The vile impostor! Providence, in its own good time, may give him a right to feast among us!" But the young man's unabashed eye dwelt upon their gloomy figures as they passed him, seeming to say, perchance with somewhat of a sneer, "First, know my secret! — then, measure your claims with mine!"

The step of Time stole onward, and soon brought merry Christmas round again, with glad and solemn worship in the churches, and sports, games, festivals, and everywhere the bright face of Joy beside the household fire. Again likewise the hall, with its curtains of dusky purple, was illuminated by the death-torches gleaming on the sepulchral decorations of the banquet. The veiled skeleton sat in state, lifting the cypress-wreath above its head, as the guerdon of some guest illustrious in the qualifications which there claimed precedence. As the stewards deemed the world inexhaustible in misery, and were desirous of recognising it in all its forms, they had not seen fit to reassemble the company of the former year. New faces now threw their gloom across the table.

There was a man of nice conscience, who bore a bloodstain in his heart — the death of a fellow-creature — which, for his more exquisite torture, had chanced with such a peculiarity of circumstances, that he could not absolutely determine whether his will had entered into the deed or not. Therefore his whole life was spent in the agony of an inward trial for murder, with a continual sifting of the details of his terrible calamity, until his mind had no longer any thought, nor his soul any emotion, disconnected with it. There was a mother, too, — a mother once, but a desolation now, — who, many years before, had gone out on a pleasure-party, and, returning, found her infant smothered in its little bed. And ever since she has been tortured with the fantasy that her buried baby lay smothering in its coffin. Then there was an aged lady, who had lived from time immemorial with a constant tremor quivering through her frame. It was terrible to discern her dark shadow tremulous upon the wall; her lips, likewise, were tremulous; and the expression of her eye seemed to indicate that her soul was trembling too. Owing to the bewilderment and confusion which made almost a chaos of her intellect, it was impossible to discover what dire misfortune had thus shaken her nature to its depths; so that the stewards had admitted her to the table, not from any acquaintance with her history, but on the safe testimony of her miserable aspect. Some surprise was expressed at the presence of a bluff, red-faced gentleman, a certain Mr. Smith, who had evidently the fat of many a rich feast within him, and the habitual twinkle of whose eye betrayed a disposition to break forth into uproarious laughter for little cause or none. It turned out, however, that, with the best possible flow of spirits, our poor friend was afflicted with a physical disease of the heart, which threatened instant death on the slightest cachinnatory indulgence, or even that titillation of the bodily frame produced by merry thoughts. In this dilemma he had sought admittance to the banquet, on the ostensible plea of his irksome and miserable state, but, in reality, with the hope of imbibing a life-preserving melancholy.

A married couple had been invited from a motive of bitter humour, it being well understood that they rendered each other unutterably miserable whenever they chanced to meet, and therefore must necessarily be fit associates at the festival. In contrast with these was another couple still unmarried, who had interchanged their hearts in early life, but had been divided by circumstances as impalpable as morning mist, and kept apart so long that their spirits now found it impossible to meet. Therefore, yearning for communion, yet shrinking from one another and choosing none beside, they felt themselves companionless in life, and looked upon eternity as a boundless desert. Next to the skeleton sat a mere son of earth, — a hunter of the Exchange, — a gatherer of shining dust, — a man whose life's record was in his ledger, and whose soul's prison-house the vaults of the bank where he kept his deposits. This person had been greatly perplexed at his invitation, deeming himself one of the most fortunate men in the city; but the stewards persisted in demanding his presence, assuring him that he had no conception how miserable he was.

And now appeared a figure which we must acknowledge as our acquaintance of the former festival. It was Gervayse Hastings, whose presence had then caused so much question and criticism, and who now took his place with the composure of one whose claims were satisfactory to himself and must needs be allowed by others. Yet his easy and unruffled face betrayed no sorrow. The well-skilled beholders gazed a moment into his eyes and shook their heads, to miss the unuttered sympathy — the countersign never to be falsified — of those whose hearts are cavern-mouths through which they descend into a region of illimitable woe and recognise other wanderers there.

"Who is this youth?" asked the man with a bloodstain on his conscience. "Surely he has never gone down into the depths! I know all the aspects of those who have passed through the dark valley. By what right is he among us?"

"Ah, it is a sinful thing to come hither without a sorrow," murmured the aged lady, in accents that partook of the eternal tremor which pervaded her whole being. "Depart, young man! Your soul has never been shaken, and, therefore, I tremble so much the more to look at you."

"His soul shaken! No; I'll answer for it," said bluff Mr Smith, pressing his hand upon his heart and making himself as melancholy as he could, for fear of a fatal explosion of laughter. "I know the lad well; he has as fair prospects as any young man about town, and has no more right among us miserable creatures than the child unborn. He never was miserable, and probably never will be!"

"Our honoured guests," interposed the stewards, "pray have patience with us, and believe, at least, that our deep veneration for the sacredness of this solemnity would preclude any wilful violation of it. Receive this young man to your table. It may not be too much to say, that no guest here would exchange his own heart for the one that beats within that youthful bosom!"

"I'd call it a bargain, and gladly, too," muttered Mr Smith, with a perplexing mixture of sadness and mirthful conceit. "A plague upon their nonsense! My own heart is the only really miserable one in the company; it will certainly be the death of me at last!"

Nevertheless, as on the former occasion, the comment of the stewards being without appeal, the company sat down. The obnoxious guest made no more attempt to obtrude his conversation on those about him, but appeared to listen to the table-talk with peculiar assiduity, as if some inestimable secret, otherwise beyond his reach, might be conveyed in a casual word. And in truth, to those who could understand and value it, there was rich matter in the upgushings and outpourings of these initiated souls to whom sorrow had been a talisman, admitting them into spiritual depths which no other spell can open. Sometimes out of the midst of densest gloom there flashed a momentary radiance, pure as crystal, bright as the flame of stars, and shedding such a glow upon the mysteries of life, that the guests were ready to exclaim, "Surely the riddle is on the point of being solved!" At such illuminated intervals the saddest mourners felt it to be revealed that mortal griefs are but shadowy and external; no more than the sable robes voluminously shrouding a certain divine reality, and thus indicating what might otherwise be altogether invisible to mortal eye.

"Just now," remarked the trembling old woman, "I

seemed to see beyond the outside. And then my everlasting tremor passed away!"

"Would that I could dwell always in these momentary gleams of light!" said the man of stricken conscience. "Then the bloodstain in my heart would be washed clean away."

This strain of conversation appeared so unintelligibly absurd to good Mr Smith, that he burst into precisely the fit of laughter which his physicians had warned him against, as likely to prove instantaneously fatal. In effect, he fell back in his chair a corpse, with a broad grin upon his face, while his ghost, perchance, remained beside it bewildered at its unpremeditated exit. This catastrophe of course broke up the festival.

"How is this? You do not tremble!" observed the tremulous old woman to Gervayse Hastings, who was gazing at the dead man with singular intentness. "Is it not awful to see him so suddenly vanish out of the midst of life, — this man of flesh and blood, whose earthly nature was no warm and strong? There is a never-ending tremor in my soul, but it trembles afresh at this! And you are calm!"

"Would that he could teach me somewhat!" said Gervayse Hastings, drawing a long breath. "Men pass before me like shadows on the wall; their actions, passions, feelings, are flickerings of the light, and then they vanish! Neither the corpse, nor yonder skeleton, nor this old woman's everlasting tremor, can give me what I seek."

And then the company departed.

We cannot linger to narrate, in such detail, more circumstances of these singular festivals, which, in accordance with the founder's will, continued to be kept with the regularity of an established institution. In process of time the stewards adopted the custom of inviting, from far and near, those individuals whose misfortunes were prominent above other men's, and whose mental and moral development might, therefore, be supposed to possess a corresponding interest. The exiled noble of the French Revolution and the broken soldier of the Empire were alike represented at the table. Fallen monarchs, wandering about the earth, have found places at that forlorn and miserable feast. The statesman, when his party flung him off, might, if he chose it, be once more a great man for the space of a single banquet. Aaron Burr's name appears on the record at a period when his ruin — the profoundest and most striking, with more of moral circumstance in it than that of almost any other man — was complete in his lonely age. Stephen Girard, when his wealth weighed upon him like a mountain, once sought admittance of his own accord. It is not probable, however, that these men had any lesson to teach in the lore of discontent and misery which might not equally well have been studied in the common walks of life. Illustrious unfortunates attract a wider sympathy, not because their griefs are more intense, but because, being set on lofty pedestals, they the better serve mankind as instances and bywords of calamity.

It concerns our present purpose to say that, at each successive festival, Gervayse Hastings showed his face, gradually changing from the smooth beauty of his youth to the thoughtful comeliness of manhood, and thence to the bald, impressive dignity of age. He was the only individual invariably present. Yet on every occasion there were murmurs, both from those who knew his character and position, and from them whose hearts shrank back as denying his companionship in their mystic fraternity.

"Who is this impassive man?" had been asked a hundred times. "Has he suffered? Has he sinned? There are no traces of either. Then wherefore is he here?"

"You must inquire of the stewards or of himself," was the constant reply. "We seem to know him well here in our city, and know nothing of him but what is creditable and fortunate. Yet hither he comes, year after year, to this gloomy banquet, and sits among the guests like a marble statue. Ask yonder skeleton, perhaps that may solve the riddle!"

It was in truth a wonder. The life of Gervayse Hastings was not merely a prosperous, but a brilliant one. Everything had gone well with him. He was wealthy, far beyond the expenditure that was required by habits of magnificence, a taste of rare purity and cultivation, a love of travel, a scholar's instinct to collect a splendid library, and, moreover, what seemed a magnificent liberality to the distressed. He had sought happiness, and not vainly, if a lovely and tender wife, and children of fair promise, could ensure it. He had, besides, ascended above the limit which separates the obscure from the distinguished, and had won a stainless reputation in affairs of the widest public importance. Not that he was a popular character, or had within him the mysterious attributes which are essential to that species of success. To the public he was a cold abstraction, wholly destitute of those rich hues of personality, that living warmth, and the peculiar faculty of stamping his own heart's impression on a multitude of hearts, by which the people recognise their favourites. And it must be owned that, after his most intimate associates had done their best to know him thoroughly, and love him warmly, they were startled to find how little hold he had upon their affections. They approved, they admired, but still in those moments when the human spirit most craves reality, they shrank back from Gervayse Hastings, as powerless to give them what they sought. It was the feeling of distrustful regret with which we should draw back the hand after extending it, in an illusive twilight, to grasp the hand of a shadow upon the wall.

As the superficial fervency of youth decayed, this peculiar effect of Gervayse Hastings's character grew more perceptible. His children, when he extended his arms, came coldly to his knees, but never climbed them of their own accord. His wife wept secretly, and almost adjudged herself a criminal because she shivered in the chill of his bosom. He, too, occasionally appeared not unconscious of the chillness of his moral atmosphere, and willing, if it might be so, to warm himself at a kindly fire. But age stole onward and benumbed him more and more. As the hoar-frost began to gather on him his wife went to her grave, and was doubtless warmer there; his children either died or were scattered to different homes of their own; and old Gervayse Hastings, unscathed by grief, — alone, but needing no companionship, — continued his steady walk through life, and still on every Christmas day attended at the dismal banquet. His privilege as a guest had become prescriptive now. Had he claimed the head of the table, even the skeleton would have been ejected from its seat.

Finally, at the merry Christmas-tide, when he had numbered fourscore years complete, this pale, high-browed, marble-featured old man once more entered the long-frequented hall, with the same impassive aspect that had called forth so much dissatisfied remark at his first attendance. Time, except in matters merely external, had done nothing for him, either of good or evil. As he took his place he threw a calm, inquiring glance around the table, as if to ascertain whether any guest had yet appeared, after so many unsuccessful banquets, who might impart to him the mystery— the deep, warm secret — the life within the life — which, whether manifested in joy or sorrow, is what gives substance to a world of shadows.

"My friends," said Gervayse Hastings, assuming a position which his long conversance with the festival caused to appear natural, "you are welcome! I drink to you all in this cup of sepulchral wine."

The guests replied courteously, but still in a manner that proved them unable to receive the old man as a member of their sad fraternity. It may be well to give the reader an idea of the present company at the banquet.

One was formerly a clergyman, enthusiastic in his profession, and apparently of the genuine dynasty of those

old Puritan divines whose faith in their calling, and stern
exercise of it, had placed them among the mighty of the
earth. But yielding to the speculative tendency of the age, he
had gone astray from the firm foundation of an ancient faith,
and wandered into a cloud-region, where everything was
misty and deceptive, ever mocking him with a semblance of
reality, but still dissolving when he flung himself upon it for
support and rest. His instinct and early training demanded
something steadfast; but, looking forward, he beheld
vapours piled on vapours, and behind him an impassable gulf
between the man of yesterday and today, on the borders of
which he paced to and fro, sometimes wringing his hands in
agony, and often making his own woe a theme of scornful
merriment. This surely was a miserable man. Next, there
was a theorist, — one of a numerous tribe, although he
deemed himself unique since the creation, — a theorist, who
had conceived a plan by which all the wretchedness of earth,
moral and physical, might be done away, and the bliss of the
millennium at once accomplished. But, the incredulity of
mankind debarring him from action, he was smitten with as
much grief as if the whole mass of woe which he was denied
the opportunity to remedy were crowded into his own
bosom. A plain old man in black attracted much of the
company's notice, on the supposition that he was no other
than Father Miller, who, it seemed, had given himself up to
despair at the tedious delay of the final conflagration. Then
there was a man distinguished for native pride and obstinacy,
who, a little while before, had possessed immense wealth,
and held the control of a vast moneyed interest which he had
wielded in the same spirit as a despotic monarch would
wield the power of his empire, carrying on a tremendous
moral warfare, the roar and tremor of which was felt at
every fireside in the land. At length came a crushing ruin, —
a total overthrow of fortune, power, and character, — the
effect of which on his imperious and, in many respects, noble
and lofty nature might have entitled him to a place, not

merely at our festival, but among the peers of Pandemonium.

There was a modern philanthropist, who had become so deeply sensible of the calamities of thousands and millions of his fellow-creatures, and of the impracticableness of any general measures for their relief, that he had no heart to do what little good lay immediately within his power, but contented himself with being miserable for sympathy. Near him sat a gentleman in a predicament hitherto unprecedented, but of which the present epoch probably affords numerous examples. Ever since he was of capacity to read a newspaper, this person had prided himself on his consistent adherence to one political party, but, in the confusion of these latter days, had got bewildered and knew not whereabouts his party was. This wretched condition, so morally desolate and disheartening to a man who has long accustomed himself to merge his individuality in the mass of a great body, can only be conceived by such as have experienced it. His next companion was a popular orator who had lost his voice, and — as it was pretty much all that he had to lose — had fallen into a state of hopeless melancholy. The table was likewise graced by two of the gentler sex, — one, a half-starved, consumptive seamstress, the representative of thousands just as wretched; the other, a women of unemployed energy, who found herself in the world with nothing to achieve, nothing to enjoy, and nothing even to suffer. She had, therefore, driven herself to the verge of madness by dark broodings over the wrongs of her sex, and its exclusion from a proper field of action. The roll of guests being thus complete, a side-table had been set for three or four disappointed office-seekers, with hearts as sick as death, whom the stewards had admitted partly because their calamities really entitled them to entrance here, and partly that they were in especial need of a good dinner. There was likewise a homeless dog, with his tail between his legs, licking up the crumbs and gnawing the fragments of the feast, — such a melancholy cur as one sometimes sees about the streets without a master, and willing to follow the first that will accept his service.

In their own way, these were as wretched a set of people as ever had assembled at the festival. There they sat, with the veiled skeleton of the founder holding aloft the cypress-wreath, at one end of the table, and at the other, wrapped in furs, the withered figure of Gervayse Hastings, stately, calm, and cold, impressing the company with awe, yet so little interesting their sympathy that he might have vanished into thin air without their once exclaiming, "Whither is he gone?"

"Sir," said the philanthropist, addressing the old man, "you have been so long a guest at this annual festival, and have thus been conversant with so many varieties of human affliction, that, not improbably, you have thence derived some great and important lessons. How blessed were your lot could you reveal a secret by which all this mass of woe might be removed!"

"I know of but one misfortune," answered Gervayse Hastings, quietly, "and that is my own."

"Your own!" rejoined the philanthropist. "And looking back on your serene and prosperous life, how can you claim to be the sole unfortunate of the human race?"

"You will not understand it," replied Gervayse Hastings, feebly, and with a singular inefficiency of pronunciation, and sometimes putting one word for another. "None have understood it, not even those who experience the like. It is a chillness, a want of earnestness, a feeling as if what should be my heart were a thing of vapour, a haunting perception of unreality! Thus seeming to possess all that other men have, all that men aim at, I have really possessed nothing, neither joy nor griefs. All things, all persons, — as was truly said to me at this table long and long ago, — have been like shadows flickering on the wall. It was so with my wife and children, with those who seemed my friends: it is so with yourselves, whom I see now before me. Neither have I myself any real existence, but am a shadow like the rest."

"And how is it with your views of a future life?" inquired the speculative clergyman.

"Worse than with you," said the old man, in a hollow and feeble tone; "for I cannot conceive it earnestly enough to feel either hope or fear. Mine, — mine is the wretchedness! This cold heart, — this unreal life! Ah! it grows colder still."

It so chanced that at this juncture the decayed ligaments of the skeleton gave way, and the dry bones fell together in a heap, thus causing the dusty wreath of cypress to drop upon the table. The attention of the company being thus diverted for a single instant from Gervayse Hastings, they perceived, on turning again towards him, that the old man had undergone a change. His shadow had ceased to flicker on the wall.

"Well, Rosina, what is your criticism?" asked Roderick, as he rolled up the manuscript.

"Frankly, your success is by no means complete," replied she. "It is true, I have an idea of the character you endeavour to describe; but it is rather by dint of my own thought than your expression."

"That is unavoidable," observed the sculptor, "because the characteristics are all negative. If Gervayse Hastings could have imbibed one human grief at the gloomy banquet, the task of describing him would have been infinitely easier. Of such persons — and we do meet with these moral monsters now and then — it is difficult to conceive how they came to exist here, or what there is in them capable of existence hereafter. They seem to be on the outside of everything; and nothing wearies the soul more than an attempt to comprehend them within its grasp."

Ambrose Bierce

THE APPLICANT

PUSHING his adventurous shins through the deep snow that had fallen overnight, and encouraged by the glee of his little sister, following in the open way that he made, a sturdy small boy, the son of Grayville's most distinguished citizen, struck his foot against something of which there was no visible sign on the surface of the snow. It is the purpose of this narrative to explain how it came to be there.

No one who had the advantage of of passing through Grayville by day can have failed to observe the large stone building crowning the low hill to the north of the railway station — that is to say, to the right in going toward Great Mowbray. It is a somewhat dull-looking edifice, of the Early Comatose order, and appears to have been designed by an architect who shrank from publicity, and although unable to conceal his work — even compelled, in this instance, to set it on an eminence in the sight of men — did what he honestly could to insure it against a second look. So far as concerns its outer and visible aspect, the Abersush Home for Old Men is unquestionably inhospitable to human attention. But it is a building of great magnitude, and cost its benevolent founder the profit of many a cargo of the teas and silks and spices that his ships brought up from the under-world when he was in trade in Boston; though the main expense was its endowment. Altogether, this reckless person had robbed his heirs-at-law of no less a sum than half a million dollars and flung it away in riotous giving.

Possibly it was with a view to get out of sight of the silent big witness to his extravagance that he shortly afterward disposed of all his Grayville property that remained to him, turned his back upon the scene of his prodigality and went off across the sea in one of his own ships. But the gossips who got their inspiration most directly from heaven declared that he went in search of a wife — a theory not easily reconciled with that of the village humorist, who solemnly averred that the bachelor philanthropist had departed this life (left Grayville, to wit) because the marriageable maidens had made it too hot to hold him. However this may have been, he had not returned, and although at long intervals there had come to Grayville, in a desultory way, vague rumours of his wanderings in strange lands, no one seemed certainly to know about him, and to the new generation he was no more than a name. But from above the portal of the Home for Old Men the name shouted in stone.

Despite its unpromising exterior, the Home is a fairly commodious place of retreat from the ills that its inmates have incurred by being poor and old and men. At the time embraced in this brief chronicle they were in number about a score, but in acerbity, querulousness, and general ingratitude they could hardly be reckoned at fewer than a hundred; at least that was the estimate of the superintendent, Mr Silas Tilbody. It was Mr Tilbody's steadfast conviction that always, in admitting new old men to replace those who had gone to another and a better Home, the trustees had distinctly in will the infraction of his peace, and the trial of his patience. In truth, the longer the institution was connected with him, the stronger was his feeling that the founder's scheme of benevolence was sadly impaired by providing any inmates at all.

He had not much imagination, but with what he had he was addicated to the reconstruction of the Home for Old Men into a kind of "castle in Spain", with himself as castellan, hospitably entertaining about a score of sleek and prosperous middle-aged gentlemen, consummately good-humoured and civilly willing to pay for their board and lodging. In this revised project of philanthropy the trustees, to whom he was indebted for his office and responsible for his conduct, had not the happiness to appear. As to them, it was held by the village humorist aforementioned that in their management of the great charity Providence had thoughtfully supplied an incentive to thrift.

With the inference which he expected to be drawn from the view we have nothing to do; it had neither support nor denial from the inmates, who certainly were most concerned. They lived out their remnant of life, crept into graves neatly numbered, and were succeeded by other old men as like them as could be desired by the Adversary of Peace. If the Home was a place of punishment for the sin of unthrift the veteran offenders sought justice with a persistence that attested the sincerity of their penitence. It is to one of these that the reader's attention is now invited.

In the matter of attire this person was not altogether engaging. But for this season, which was mid-winter, a careless observer might have looked upon him as a clever device of the husbandman indisposed to share the fruits of his toil with the crows that toil not, neither spin — an error that might not have been dispelled without longer and closer observation than he seemed to court; for his progress up Abersush Street, toward the Home in the gloom of the winter evening, was not visibly faster than what might have been expected of a scarecrow blessed with youth, health, and discontent. The man was indisputably ill-clad, yet not without a certain fitness and good taste withal; for he was obviously an applicant for admittance to the Home, where poverty was a qualification. In the army of indigence the uniform is rags; they serve to distinguish the rank and file from the recruiting officers.

As the old man, entering the gate of the grounds, shuffled up the broad walk, already white with the fast-falling snow, which from time to time he feebly shook from its various coigns of vantage on his person, he came under inspection of the large globe lamp that burned always by night over the great door of the building. As if unwilling to incur its revealing beams he turned to the left and, passing a considerable distance along the face of the building, rang at a smaller door emitting a dimmer ray that came from within, through the fanlight, and expended itself incuriously overhead. The door was opened by no less than the great Mr Tilbody himself. Observing his visitor, who at once uncovered, and somewhat shortened the radius of the permanent curvature of his back, the great man gave visible token of neither surprise nor displeasure. Mr Tilbody was, indeed, in an uncommonly good humour, a phenomenon ascribable doubtless to the cheerful influence of the season; for this was Christmas Eve, and the morrow would be that blessed 365th part of the year that all Christian souls set apart for mighty feats of goodness and joy.

Mr Tilbody was so full of the spirit of the season that his fat face and pale blue eyes, whose ineffectual fire served to distinguish it from an untimely summer squash, effused so genial a glow that it seemed a pity that he could not have lain down in it, basking in the consciousness of his own identity. He was hatted, booted, overcoated, and umbrellaed, as became a person who was about to expose himself to the night and the storm on an errand of charity; for Mr Tilbody had just parted from his wife and children to go "down town" and purchase the wherewithal to confirm the annual flasehood about the hunch-bellied saint who frequents the chimneys to reward little boys and girls who are good, and especially truthful. So he did not invite the old man in, but saluted him cheerily:

"Hello! Just in time; a moment later and you would have missed me. Come, I have no time to waste; we'll walk a little way together."

"Thank you," said the old man, upon whose thin and

white but ignoble face the light from the open door showed an expression that was perhaps disappointment; "but if the trustees — if my application ——"

"The trustees," Mr Tilbody said, closing more doors than one, and cutting off two kinds of light, "have agreed that your application disagrees with them."

Certain sentiments are inappropriate to Christmastide, but Humour, like Death, has all seasons for his own.

"Oh, my God!" cried the old man, in so thin and husky a tone that the invocation was anything but impressive, and to at least one of his two auditors sounded, indeed, somewhat ludicrous. To the Other — but that is a matter which laymen are devoid of the light to expound.

"Yes," continued Mr Tilbody, accommodating his gait to that of his companion, who was mechanically, and not very successfully, retracing the track that he had made through the snow; "they have decided that under the circumstances — under the very peculiar circumstances, you understand — it would be inexpedient to admit you. As superintendent and *ex officio* secretary of the honourable board" — as Mr Tilbody "read his title clear" the magnitude of the big building, seen through its veil of falling snow, appeared to be suffering somewhat in comparison — "it is my duty to inform you that, in the words of Deacon Bryan, the chairman, your presence in the Home would — under the circumstances — be peculiarly embarrassing. I felt it my duty to present to the honourable board the statement that you made to me yesterday of your needs, your physical condition, and the trials which it has pleased Providence to send upon you in your very proper effort to present your claims in person; but, after careful, and I may say prayerful, consideration of your case — with something too, I trust, of the large charitableness appropriate to the season — it was decided that we would not be justified in doing anything likely to impair the usefulness of the institution entrusted (under Providence) to our care."

They had now passed out of the grounds; the street lamp opposite the gate was dimly visible through the snow. Already the old man's former track was obliterated, and he seemed uncertain as to which way he should go. Mr Tilbody had drawn a little away from him, and paused and turned half toward him, apparently reluctant to forego the continuing opportunity.

"Under the circumstances," he resumed, "the decision——"

But the old man was inaccessible to the suasion of his verbosity; he had crossed the street into a vacant lot and was going forward, rather deviously, toward nowhere in particular — which, he having nowhere in particular to go, was not so reasonless a proceeding as it looked.

And that is how it happened that the next morning, when the church bells of all Grayville were ringing with an unction appropriate to the day, the sturdy little son of Deacon Bryan, breaking a way through the snow to the place of worship, struck his foot against the body of Amasa Abersush, philanthropist.

Guy De Maupassant

CHRISTMAS EVE

"THE Christmas-eve supper! Oh! no, I shall never go in for that again!" Stout Henri Templier said that in a furious voice, as if someone had proposed some crime to him, while the others laughed and said:

"What are you flying into a rage about?"

"Because a Christmas-eve supper played me the dirtiest trick in the world, and ever since I have felt an insurmountable horror for that night of imbecile gaiety."

"Tell us about it."

"You want to know what it was? Very well then, just listen.

"You remember how cold it was two years ago at Christmas; cold enough to kill poor people in the streets. The Seine was covered with ice; the pavements froze one's feet through the soles of one's boots, and the whole world seemed to be at the point of congealing.

"I had a big piece of work on, and refused every invitation to supper, as I preferred to spend the night at my writing table. I dined alone and then began to work. But about ten o'clock I grew restless at the thought of the gay and busy life all over Paris, at the noise in the streets which reached me in spite of everything, at my neighbours' preparations for supper, which I heard through the walls. I hardly knew any longer what I was doing; I wrote nonsense, and at last I came to the conclusion that I had better give up all hope of producing any good work that night.

"I walked up and down my room; I sat down and got up again. I was certainly under the mysterious influence of the enjoyment outside, and I resigned myself to it. So I rang for my servant, and said to her:

"'Angela, go and get a good supper for two; some oysters, a cold partridge, some crayfish, ham, and some cakes. Put out two bottles of champagne, lay the cloth and go to bed.'

"She obeyed in some surprise, and when all was ready, I put on my greatcoat and went out. The great question remained: 'Whom was I going to bring in to supper?' My female friends had all been invited elsewhere, and if I had wished to have one, I ought to have seen about it beforehand. So I thought that I would do a good action at the same time, and said to myself:

"'Paris is full of poor and pretty girls who will have nothing on the table tonight, and who are on the lookout for some generous fellow. I will act the part of Providence to one of them this evening; and I will find one if I have to go to every pleasure resort and I will hunt till I find one to my choice.' So I started off on my search.

"I certainly found many poor girls who were on the lookout for some adventure, but they were ugly enough to give a man a fit of indigestion, or thin enough to freeze in their tracks if they stopped, and you all know that I have a weakness for stout women. The more flesh they have, the better I like them, and a female colossus would be my ideal.

"Suddenly, opposite the 'Théâtre des Variétés', I saw a figure to my liking. I trembled with pleasure, and said:

"'By jove! What a fine girl!'

"It only remained for me to see her face, for a woman's face is the dessert.

"I hastened on, overtook her, and turned round suddenly under a gas lamp. She was charming, quite young, dark, with large, black eyes, and I immediately made my proposition which she accepted without any hesitation, and a quarter of an hour later we were sitting at supper in my lodgings. 'Oh!

how comfortable it is here,' she said as she came in, and looked about her with evident satisfaction at having found a supper and a bed on that bitter night. She was superb; so beautiful that she astonished me, and so stout that she fairly captivated me.

"She took off her cloak and hat, sat down and began to eat; but she seemed in low spirits, and sometimes her pale face twitched as if she were suffering from hidden sorrow.

" 'Have you anything troubling you?' I asked her.

" 'Bah! Don't let us think of troubles!'

"And she began to drink. She emptied her champagne glass at a draught, filled it again, and emptied it again, without stopping, and soon a little colour came into her cheeks and she began to laugh.

"I adored her already, kissed her continually, and discovered that she was neither stupid, nor common, nor coarse as ordinary street-walkers are. I asked her for some details about her life, but she replied:

" 'My little fellow, that is no business of yours!' Alas! an hour later!

"At last it was time to retire, and while I was clearing the table, which had been laid in front of the fire, she undressed herself quickly, and got in. My neighbours were making a terrible din, singing and laughing like lunatics, and so I said to myself:

" 'I was quite right to go out and bring in this girl; I should never have been able to do any work.'

"At this moment, however, a deep groan made me look around, and I said:

" 'What is the matter with you, my dear?'

"She did not reply, but continued to utter painful sighs, as if she were suffering horribly, and I continued:

" 'Do you feel ill?' And suddenly she uttered a cry, a heart-rending cry, and I rushed up to the bed, with a candle in my hand.

"Her face was distorted with pain, and she was wringing

her hands, panting and uttering long, deep groans, which sounded like a rattle in the throat, and were painful to hear. I asked her in consternation:

"'What is the matter with you? Do tell me what is the matter.'

"'Oh! the pain! the pain!' she said. I pulled up the bed-clothes, and I saw, my friends, that she was in labour.

"Then I lost my head, and ran and knocked at the wall with my fists, shouting: 'Help! help!'

"My door was opened almost immediately, and a crowd of people came in, men in evening clothes, women in full dress, harlequins, Turks, musketeers, and the inroad startled me so, that I could not explain myself, while they who had thought that some accident had happened or that a crime had been committed, could not understand what was the matter. At last, however, I managed to say:

"'This — this — woman — is being confined.'

"Then they looked at her, and gave their opinion. A friar, especially, declared that he knew all about it, and wished to assist nature, but as they were all as drunk as pigs I was afraid that they would kill her. So I rushed downstairs without my hat, to fetch an old doctor, who lived in the next street. When I came back with him, the whole house was up; the gas on the stairs had been relighted, the lodgers from every floor were in my room, while four boatmen were finishing my champagne and crayfish.

"As soon as they saw me they raised a loud shout. A milkmaid presented me with a horrible little wrinkled specimen of humanity, that was mewing like a cat, and said to me:

"'It is a girl.'

"The doctor examined the woman, declared that she was in a dangerous state, as the event had occurred immediately after supper, and took his leave, saying he would immediately send a sick nurse and a wet nurse. An hour later, the two women came, bringing all that was requisite with them.

"I spent the night in my armchair, too distracted to be able to think of the consequences, and almost as soon as it was light the doctor came again. He found his patient very ill, and said to me:

" 'Your wife, Monsieur—'

" 'She is not my wife,' I interrupted him.

" 'Very well then, your mistress; it does not matter to me.'

"He told me what must be done for her, what her diet must be, and then wrote a prescription.

"What was I to do? Could I send the poor creature to the hospital? I should have been looked upon as a brute in the house and in all the neighbourhood. So I kept her in my rooms, and she had my bed for six weeks.

"I sent the child to some peasants at Poissy to be taken care of, and she still costs me fifty francs a month, for as I had paid at first, I shall be obliged to go on paying as long as I live. Later on, she will believe that I am her father. But to crown my misfortunes, when the girl had recovered, I found that she was in love with me, madly in love with me, the baggage!"

"Well?"

"Well, she had grown as thin as a homeless cat, and I turned the skeleton out of doors. But she watches for me in the streets, hides herself, so that she may see me pass, stops me in the evening when I go out, in order to kiss my hand, and, in fact, worries me enough to drive me mad. That is why I never keep Christmas eve now."

Anon.

A CHRISAMASS PYE

OR ENTERTAINMENT FOR THE *YOLE* VACANCE

HAPPYNESS is the Mark every one Levels at, it being a Principle in Nature to Aspire at Felicitie but through the Darkness of the Understanding Corruptions of the Will, most Men either mistake the Mark, by placeing Happiness in rheigs [things(?)] wherein it is not to be found, or else tho they do not Err in the Object, mistake the means whereby it is attained.

From hence arise not only Different Opinions, as to the Object of Addorration, but innumberable Modes, Rites, and Cerminonies in the manner, time and other Circumstances of Worship.

One Man Esteemeth one *Day* to be more Holy then another, another Man Esteemeth all Days alike, and in particular this Day called *Christmass*, or the day of the Nativity of our Blessed LORD, is Reckoned by many worthy to be Celebrat or set a part in a particular manner for that Reason.

The chief grounds or Arguments made use of for the Celebration of this day, are gathered from the Practice of the Church of the *Jews*, who by Divine appointment were Commanded to Solemnize several Anniversary Days, from whence it is inferred that the Christians are no less oblidged to Commemerat the Memerable Days wherein they have

Received Singular Blessings, of which the Nativity of our Blessed LORD is the chief.

To Fortfie and Strenthen this Opinion, the Change of the Sabbath from the Seventh to the first Day of the week, and the Initiating Sacrament of Baptisim for Circumcision, both of Divine Constitution, is made use of as an Argument to shew the Reasonableness of Substituting Christian Feastivals in Roum of these solomnized by the *Jewish* Church.

On the other Hand these who do not think they ought to Solemnize Aniversar-*Days*, Justify their Opnion by Denying a power in the Church, Except upon Emargincys, that Require immediate Humiliation or Thanksgivings, without an Express Divine Precep, lest they should be found guilty of will Worship and Superstition, it being Espreslie Required of us. *That we do not any thing shet to Kight* [that is Right(?)] *in our own Eyes; But that which the LORD thy GOD Commandeth thee that shalt thou do.* And from the History of the Scriptures It is Notour, that such Practices are highly offensive in the Sight of GOD, and frequentlie Reproved by the Prophets, in these or the like words, *Who hath Required those things at your Hand?* And therefore think it better to take the infalable Word of Truth for their Rule, then the Aathority of the Church, how Specious soever the Pretext may be, and the intention never so Good.

The Nativity, Resurrection and Ascension of our Blessed LORD are inesteemable Mercies to an Elect world; But since the Divine Wisdom has not thought fit to injoyn the Aniversary Celebration of these Days on which these Events, happened, what Human Power dare appoint it?

Besides the Days of our Blessed LORDs Nativitie is not Certainlie known. No-thing in the whole Scriptures of Truth (our only Rule) doth assertain it, nor are Men well agreed in Human Testimonies about it, and it must be very strange to believe that GOD would have left us in the Dark even as to the perceise Day if he had thought fit it should be Actualy Comemorate.

Moreover the Example of the *Jewish* Church in their Anual Feastivals is Exceeding Lame to bear the Conclusion they draw from it. That the *Jews* observed Anual Feastivals to Comemorat Memorial Events, therefore the Christians ought to do so too, not minding that the *Jews* had an Express Command for their Practice, and the standing precep not Abrogat by CHRIST or his Apostles by any Subsequent Institution. *Not what seemeth right in thy own Eyes, but what the LORD thy GOD Commands thee that shalt thou do*, still Stairing them in the Faces.

The other part of the Argument is no better founded, Viz. That because those who cannot conform to the Solmenizing of Aniversary Days, own the Authority of the Church in Substituting Baptisem in the Roum of Circumcision, and the change of the Sabbath from the Seventh to the first Day of the Week, they must likewise approve of the Christian Feastivals in place of the *Jewish* or be in consistant with themselves, Such as are before Hand determine and would have the Rule made conformable to their practice instead of conforming their Practice to the Rule, many think this Argument of Force; But when it is weighted in the Ballance of the Sanctuary it will be found to be as Light as Vanity it self.

To Compare these Cases they alledge to be paralel let us see upon what grounds the Sabbath was Changed, the Scriptures are Express, that the Apostles set a part one Day of Seven for the Service of God, without Restricting it to the Seventh Day of the Week. But there is not one Sylable in all the New Testament injoyning the Celebration of CHRISTS Birth Day, or any other Aniversary Solemnity either by way of Preceep, or mentioned in the Example of the Church.

Baptism is Expreslie Commanded, and mention is made of Baptising whole Families, wherein it is probable there were several Infants. But there is no precept injoyning the keeping of CHRISTS Nativity, if their had, the Dispute about the preceise Days had not been so material, as the institution of the thing it self, without the least shadow of Divine Authority.

The Aniversary Feasts of the *Jews* were all by Express Precept (except that in Comemoration of their Deliverance from *Hamans* Plot, which is mentioned in the History of the Scriptures) but whither by way of Aprobation is more I suppose than can be wel proven. And besides these Aniversary Feasts were not only for Comemorating Singal Events, but had a Referance to the Spiritual Benefits thereby Tyipified and held forth, as all their Washings and External Purifications, were Typical of Spiritual Purity and Holyness; But it is not so in the Gospel Oeconemie, which Requires only Spiritual Worship.

Can any Man think he Honours GOD by filling his Belly with good Meat (and it were well if many went not further) even to Roing and Drunkness, if not also to other gross Acts of imorality, Gaming, and Swearing, &c. As the Prophet *Isaiah* sayeth to a Superstitious People made upon their own Inventions; Is this the Fast that you have Chosen? It may be said, is this the Feast that you have Chosen? and he Proceeds to tell them of another kind of behaviour that would be acceptable Service to God, and our Blessed Lord say, to a Supersticious People in this Day, *well did Elaios Prophesie of you, this People draw near to me with the Mouth but are far from me with their Harts.*

But because the Advocats for this Cause pretend, they do not approve of the Abuse of this Day, by such Extravigancey, and Require only at their Prososits, a Devot keeping of it, (which I wish they would observe) yet I must Remarke one thing from it, Viz. That when People have formed a Schem of Worship of their own Divising which they think will be acceptable to GOD Commonly (if not always) the design is perverted, in the Practice of their Prosolits, and no wonder, that these who do not closlie abide by the Rule perscribed by GOD, cannot abide by that Devised by themselves.

Editors' Note: The original spelling in this document has been retained by us where it does not seriously stand in the way of comprehension. The original typography, which often varies from letter to letter, involves many printer's errors, of which "u" for "n" or vice versa was perhaps the most frequent; we have in most instances returned these to the meaning intended, when it could be discovered. A few readings are conjectural. A copy of the original printed text is to be found in the National Library of Scotland, which adds to the internal evidence that the author was a Scot.

The Gospel according to

ST. LUKE

CHAPTER I

FORASMUCH as many have taken in hand to set forth in order a declaration of those things which are most surely believed among us,

2 Even as they delivered them unto us, which from the beginning were eyewitnesses, and ministers of the word;

3 It seemed good to me also, having had perfect understanding of all things from the very first, to write unto thee in order, most excellent Theophilus,

4 That thou mightest know the certainty of those things, wherein thou hast been instructed.

5 There was in the days of Herod, the king of Judæa, a certain priest named Zacharias, of the course of Abia: and his wife *was* of the daughters of Aaron, and her name *was* Elisabeth.

6 And they were both righteous before God, walking in all the commandments and ordinances of the Lord blameless.

7 And they had no child, because that Elisabeth was barren, and they both were *now* well stricken in years.

8 And it came to pass, that while he executed the priest's office before God in the order of his course,

9 According to the custom of the priest's office, his lot was to burn incense when he went into the temple of the Lord.

10 And the whole multitude of the people were praying without at the time of incense.

11 And there appeared unto him an angel of the Lord standing on the right side of the altar of incense.

12 And when Zacharias saw *him*, he was troubled, and fear fell upon him.

13 But the angel said unto him, Fear not, Zacharias: for thy prayer is heard; and thy wife Elisabeth shall bear thee a son, and thou shalt call his name John.

14 And thou shalt have joy and gladness; and many shall rejoice at his birth.

15 For he shall be great in the sight of the Lord, and shall drink neither wine nor strong drink; and he shall be filled with the Holy Ghost, even from his mother's womb.

16 And many of the children of Israel shall he turn to the Lord their God.

17 And he shall go before him in the spirit and power of Elias, to turn the hearts of the fathers to the children, and the disobedient to the wisdom of the just; to make ready a people prepared for the Lord.

18 And Zacharias said unto the angel, Whereby shall I know this? for I am an old man, and my wife well stricken in years.

19 And the angel answering said unto him, I am Gabriel, that stand in the presence of God; and am sent to speak unto thee, and to shew thee these glad tidings.

20 And, behold, thou shalt be dumb, and not able to speak, until the day that these things shall be performed, because thou believest not my words, which shall be fulfilled in their season.

21 And the people waited for Zacharias, and marvelled that he tarried so long in the temple.

22 And when he came out, he could not speak unto them: and they perceived that he had seen a vision in the temple: for he beckoned unto them, and remained speechless.

23 And it came to pass, that, as soon as the days of his ministration were accomplished, he departed to his own house.

24 And after those days his wife Elisabeth conceived, and hid herself five months, saying,

25 Thus hath the Lord dealt with me in the days wherein he looked on *me*, to take away my reproach among men.

26 And in the sixth month the angel Gabriel was sent from God unto a city of Galilee, named Nazareth,

27 To a virgin espoused to a man whose name was Joseph, of the house of David; and the virgin's name *was* Mary.

28 And the angel came in unto her, and said, Hail, *thou that art* highly favoured, the Lord *is* with thee: blessed *art* thou among women.

29 And when she saw *him*, she was troubled at his saying, and cast in her mind what manner of salutation this should be.

30 And the angel said unto her, Fear not, Mary: for thou has found favour with God.

31 And, behold, thou shalt conceive in thy womb, and bring forth a son, and shalt call his name JESUS.

32 He shall be great, and shall be called the Son of the Highest: and the Lord God shall give unto him the throne of his father David:

33 And he shall reign over the house of Jacob for ever; and of his kingdom there shall be no end.

34 Then said Mary unto the angel, How shall this be, seeing I know not a man?

35 And the angel answered and said unto her, The Holy Ghost shall come upon thee, and the power of the Highest shall overshadow thee: therefore also that holy thing which shall be born of thee shall be called the Son of God.

36 And, behold, thy cousin Elisabeth, she hath also conceived a son in her old age: and this is the sixth month with her, who was called barren.

37 For with God nothing shall be impossible.

38 And Mary said, Behold the handmaid of the Lord; be it unto me according to thy word. And the angel departed from her.

39 And Mary arose in those days, and went into the hill country with haste, into a city of Juda;

40 And entered into the house of Zacharias, and saluted Elisabeth.

41 And it came to pass, that, when Elisabeth heard the salutation of Mary, the babe leaped in her womb; and Elisabeth was filled with the Holy Ghost:

42 And she spake out with a loud voice, and said, Blessed *art* thou among women, and blessed *is* the fruit of thy womb.

43 And whence *is* this to me, that the mother of my Lord should come to me?

44 For, lo, as soon as the voice of thy salutation sounded in mine ears, the babe leaped in my womb for joy.

45 And blessed *is* she that believed: for there shall be a performance of those things which were told her from the Lord.

46 And Mary said, My soul doth magnify the Lord,

47 And my spirit hath rejoiced in God my Saviour.

48 For he hath regarded the low estate of his handmaiden: for, behold, from henceforth all generations shall call me blessed.

49 For he that is mighty hath done to me great things; and holy *is* his name.

50 And his mercy *is* on them that fear him from generation to generation.

51 He hath shewed strength with his arm; he hath scattered the proud in the imagination of their hearts.

52 He hath put down the mighty from *their* seats, and exalted them of low degree.

53 He hath filled the hungry with good things; and the rich he hath sent empty away.

54 He hath holpen his servant Israel, in remembrance of *his* mercy;

55 As he spake to our fathers, to Abraham, and to his seed for ever.

56 And Mary abode with her about three months, and returned to her own house.

57 Now Elisabeth's full time came that she should be delivered; and she brought forth a son.

58 And her neighbours and her cousins heard how the Lord had shewed great mercy upon her; and they rejoiced with her.

59 And it came to pass, that on the eighth day they came to circumcise the child; and they called him Zacharias, after the name of his father.

60 And his mother answered and said, Not *so*; but he shall be called John.

61 And they said unto her, There is none of thy kindred that is called by this name.

62 And they made signs to his father, how he would have him called.

63 And he asked for a writing table, and wrote, saying, His name is John. And they marvelled all.

64 And his mouth was opened immediately, and his tongue *loosed*, and he spake, and praised God.

65 And fear came on all that dwelt round about them: and all these sayings were noised abroad throughout all the hill country of Judæa.

66 And all they that heard *them* laid *them* up in their hearts, saying, What manner of child shall this be! And the hand of the Lord was with him.

67 And his father Zacharias was filled with the Holy Ghost, and prophesied, saying,

68 Blessed *be* the Lord God of Israel; for he hath visited and redeemed his people,

69 And hath raised up an horn of salvation for us in the house of his servant David;

70 As he spake by the mouth of his holy prophets, which have been since the world began:

71 That we should be saved from our enemies, and from the hand of all that hate us;

72 To perform the mercy *promised* to our fathers, and to remember his holy covenant;

73 The oath which he sware to our father Abraham,

74 That he would grant unto us, that we being delivered out of the hand of our enemies might serve him without fear,

75 In holiness and righteousness before him, all the days of our life.

76 And thou, child, shalt be called the prophet of the Highest: for thou shalt go before the face of the Lord to prepare his ways;

77 To give knowledge of salvation unto his people by the remission of their sins,

78 Through the tender mercy of our God; whereby the dayspring from on high hath visited us,

79 To give light to them that sit in darkness and *in* the shadow of death, to guide our feet into the way of peace.

80 And the child grew, and waxed strong in spirit, and was in the desert till the day of his shewing unto Israel.

CHAPTER II

AND it came to pass in those days, that there went out a decree from Cæsar Augustus, that all the world should be taxed.

2 (*And* this taxing was first made when Cyrenius was governor of Syria.)

3 And all went to be taxed, every one into his own city.

4 And Joseph also went up from Galilee, out of the city of Nazareth, into Judæa, unto the city of David, which is called Bethlehem; (because he was of the house and lineage of David:)

5 To be taxed with Mary his espoused wife, being great with child.

6 And so it was, that, while they were there, the days were accomplished that she should be delivered.

7 And she brought forth his first born son, and wrapped him in swaddling clothes, and laid him in a manger; because there was no room for them in the inn.

8 And there were in the same country shepherds abiding in the field, keeping watch over their flock by night.

9 And, lo, the angel of the Lord came upon them, and the glory of the Lord shone round about them: and they were sore afraid.

10 And the angel said unto them, Fear not: for, behold, I bring you good tidings of great joy, which shall be to all people.

11 For unto you is born this day in the city of David a Saviour, which is Christ the Lord.

12 And this *shall be* a sign unto you; Ye shall find the babe wrapped in swaddling clothes, lying in a manger.

13 And suddenly there was with the angel a multitude of the heavenly host praising God, and saying,

14 Glory to God in the highest, and on earth peace, good will toward men.

15 And it came to pass, as the angels were gone away from them into heaven, the shepherds said one to another, Let us now go even unto Bethlehem, and see this thing which is come to pass, which the Lord hath made known unto us.

16 And they came with haste, and found Mary, and Joseph, and the babe lying in a manger.

17 And when they had seen *it*, they made known abroad the saying which was told them concerning this child.

18 And all they that heard *it* wondered at those things which were told them by the shepherds.

19 But Mary kept all these things, and pondered *them* in her heart.

20 And the shepherds returned, glorifying and praising God for all the things that they had heard and seen, as it was told unto them.

21 And when eight days were accomplished for the circumcising of the child, his name was called JESUS, which

was so named of the angel before he was conceived in the womb.

22 And when the days of her purification according to the law of Moses were accomplished, they brought him to Jerusalem, to present *him* to the Lord;

23 (As it is written in the law of the Lord, Every male that openeth the womb shall be called holy to the Lord;)

24 And to offer a sacrifice according to that which is said in the law of the Lord, A pair of turtledoves, or two young pigeons.

25 And, behold, there was a man in Jerusalem, whose name *was* Simeon; and the same man *was* just and devout, waiting for the consolation of Israel: and the Holy Ghost was upon him.

26 And it was revealed unto him by the Holy Ghost, that he should not see death, before he had seen the Lord's Christ.

27 And he came by the spirit into the temple: and when the parents brought in the child Jesus, to do for him after the custom of the law,

28 Then took he him up in his arms, and blessed God, and said,

29 Lord, now lettest thou thy servant depart in peace, according to thy word:

30 For mine eyes have seen thy salvation,

31 Which thou hast prepared before the face of all people;

32 A light to lighten the Gentiles, and the glory of thy people Israel.

33 And Joseph and his mother marvelled at those things which were spoken of him.

34 And Simeon blessed them, and said unto Mary his mother, Behold, this *child* is set for the fall and rising again of many in Israel; and for a sign which shall be spoken against;

35 (Yea, a sword shall pierce through thy own soul also,) that the thoughts of many hearts may be revealed.

36 And there was one Anna, a prophetess, the daughter of Phanuel, of the tribe of Aser: she was of a great age, and had

lived with an husband seven years from her virginity;

37 And she *was* a widow of about fourscore and four years, which departed not from the temple, but served *God* with fastings and prayers night and day.

38 And she coming in that instant gave thanks likewise unto the Lord, and spake of him to all them that looked for redemption in Jerusalem.

39 And when they had performed all things according to the law of the Lord, they returned into Galilee, to their own city of Nazareth.

40 And the child grew, and waxed strong in spirit, filled with wisdom: and the grace of God was upon him.

41 Now his parents went to Jerusalem every year at the feast of the passover.

42 And when he was twelve years old, they went up to Jerusalem after the custom of the feast.

43 And when they had fulfilled the days, as they returned, the child Jesus tarried behind in Jerusalem; and Joseph and his mother knew not *of it*.

44 But they, supposing him to have been in the company, went a day's journey; and they sought him among *their* kinsfolk and acquaintance.

45 And when they found him not, they turned back again to Jerusalem, seeking him.

46 And it came to pass, that after three days they found him in the temple, sitting in the midst of the doctors, both hearing them, and asking them questions.

47 And all that heard him were astonished at his understanding and answers.

48 And when they saw him, they were amazed: and his mother said unto him, Son, why hast thou thus dealt with us? behold, thy father and I have sought thee sorrowing.

49 And he said unto them, How is it that ye sought me? wist ye not that I must be about my Father's business?

50 And they understood not the saying which he spake unto them.

51 And he went down with them, and came to Nazareth, and was subject unto them: but his mother kept all these sayings in her heart.

52 And Jesus increased in wisdom and stature, and in favour with God and man.

A NOTE ON THE CONTENTS

JOHN Milton (1608-74) was still at Cambridge University when he wrote his ode *On the Morning of Christs Nativity* for Christmas 1629, but had received his bachelor's degree earlier that year.

The Gaelic poem *Oidche nam Bannag* (Christmas Eve) here given only in translation, was transcribed from Roderick MacNeill, a cottar, of Mingulay, Barra; he would have learned it in the nineteenth century but it is clearly much older.

"I come from heuin to tell" reflects the mood of Scottish Protestant episcopalianism in which it was written early in the Scottish Reformation.

"Preparations" survives in a manuscript copy preserved at Christ Church College, Oxford, and is probably from the seventeenth century.

The "Nativitie" of John Donne (1573-1631) is one of the *Divine Poems* probably written in 1607, when he sent them to Lady Magdalen Herbert.

Hugh MacDiarmid's "The Innumerable Christ" is one of the poems in his *Sangschaw* (1925), the collection in which he first expressed his lifelong concern to assert the vitality of the Scottish tongue Lallans; his earlier work was largely under his own name, Christopher Murray Grieve (1892-1978).

Anthony Ross is a Scottish preacher, penologist, historian, critic and Dominican priest, born in 1917. "Christ Ran Stumbling" was written in 1937-38, and first appeared in *Scottish Verse 1851-1951*, edited by Douglas Young (1952).

Conor Cruise O'Brien, born in 1917 in Dublin, was editor-in-chief of the *Observer* when his "Long Day's Journey Into Prayer" appeared there on 4th February 1979. His *States of Ireland*, while reflecting his historical, cultural and political interests, includes further material on his family background.

Gilbert Keith Chesterton (1874-1936) wrote his first six stories about Father Brown with extraordinary rapidity, "The Flying Stars" being the fourth. With six others they appeared in 1911 as *The Innocence of Father Brown*, and reflected his sympathies with Catholicism although he did not become a Roman Catholic until well after another decade.

Robert Louis Stevenson (1850-94) wrote "Markheim" in Bournemouth in 1885, and it represents a rejection of the Calvinistic predestinarianism of his native Edinburgh; "Christmas at Sea" was composed in 1888 when he had gone to the South Seas whence he would never return.

Rudyard Kipling (1865-1936) wrote "Christmas in India" in 1885 or 1886 and was thoroughly delighted when it was parodied by Kay Robinson's "Christmas in England" which appeared alongside it in an Indian paper, the *Pioneer*, becoming the foundation of their friendship.

Arthur Conan Doyle (1859-1930) was still a struggling doctor with memories of a year in the Jesuit college at Feldkirch in Germany when he wrote "An Exciting Christmas Eve"; published in the Christmas number of the *Boy's Own Paper* for 1883; this is its first book publication.

Pelham Grenville Wodehouse (1881-1975) had twenty years of professional writing behind him when "Sundered Hearts" was published in *The Clicking of Cuthbert* in 1922 but the volume represents his earliest mature work in the short story, specifically in its satire of contemporary literary fashions.

Enoch Arnold Bennett (1867-1931) was still experimenting with
varieties of fiction, including the exotic thriller, when he turned to
his native potteries of Staffordshire for *The Grim Smile of the Five
Towns* in 1907; it contains "Vera's First Christmas Adventure"
with two sequels, and anticipates his famous novels based in the
same world.

Hector Hugh Munro (1870-1916) produced his "Reginald"
sketches and stories in the earliest years of Edward VII's reign
although his major short stories belong to that of George V until
the war in which he died. His pseudonym "Saki" was borrowed
from the Ganymede of the *Rubaiyat* of Omar Khayyam.

Professor Stephen Butler Leacock (1869-1944), English-born but
long Canadian-domiciled, was head of the Economics Department at McGill University, Montreal, and author of *Elements of
Political Science* (1906) when he began his major humorous writing
with *Literary Lapses* (1910) where "A Christmas Letter" appeared;
he followed it with his two other masterpieces, *Nonsense Novels* and
Sunshine Sketches of a Little Town, in successive years.

The diary of Samuel Pepys (1633-1703) was only kept by the great
naval administrator for the years of the 1660s, after which his sight
gave way, and it remained unknown until the nineteenth century,
nor was its text finally established until R. C. Latham's edition in
recent years.

The gentlest and most humane satire of early eighteenth-century
England is to be found in the work of Joseph Addison (1672-1719) in
the *Spectator*, although the characters first owed life to the cruder
hand of his colleague Richard Steele. Sir Roger de Coverley's
views on Christmas were given to the *Spectator*'s readers on
Tuesday, 8th January 1712 (no. 269).

Thomas Babington Macaulay (1800-59) above all intended his
History of England, in whose second chapter the Christmas passage
appears, to be an intermingling of political and social history; his
last surviving letter, written on Christmas Day 1859 to his friend
Thomas Flower Ellis, expressed a yearning for the death which
followed a few days later.

"All Quiet for Christmas" was given to us as a copy from a contemporary newspaper. It is unlikely that the popular writer Piers Compton wrote it until the 1920s, as he was not born until 1903; it reflects his Roman Catholic convictions as well as the anti-war mood of the early 1920s, although it specifically harks back to hostility to the war in 1914.

Percy Mackaye (1875-1956), son of the actor-director Steele Mackaye, was an American but his cosmopolitan cultural background and extensive travel in Europe led to his involvement in the European war before the United States entered it in 1917.

Thomas Michael Kettle (1880-1916), an Irish politician and economist (and uncle of Conor Cruise O'Brien), fought on the British side in World War I and his "To My Daughter Betty" evidently foresees the death that found him four days later.

Thomas Hardy (1840-1928) has been somewhat overshadowed as a poet by his great Wessex novels, but is coming to be recognised as one of the foremost poetic witnesses to the origins, course and aftermath of the Great War other than those who took part in it.

Nathaniel Hawthorne (1804-64), the great literary anatomist of his New England Puritan heritage, published "The Christmas Banquet" in 1846 as one of the offerings in his *Mosses from an old Manse*.

Ambrose Gwinnett Bierce, born in 1842, apparently wrote "The Applicant" in or shortly before 1891, when it appeared in the first (San Francisco) edition of his *Tales of Soldiers and Civilians*, but it was omitted when the book was published in London the following year under its more famous title *In the Midst of Life*. The reason for the discrepancy is, like the date of the author's death, unknown.

Guy de Maupassant (1850-93) included "Nuit de Noel" (here translated as "Christmas Eve") in the second edition of his *Mademoiselle Fifi*, which appeared in 1883, but it was not present in the previous edition of 1882.

A Chrisamass Pye is preserved in two execrably-printed broad-sheets in the National Library of Scotland, to whose admirable catalogue we are indebted for it.

The opening chapters of St. Luke's Gospel are taken from the King James Authorised Version of the Bible.